Political Film

The Dialectics of Third Cinema

Mike Wayne

Pluto Press

LONDON • STERLING, VIRGINIA

First published 2001 by Pluto Press
345 Archway Road, London N6 5AA
and 22883 Quicksilver Drive,
Sterling, VA 20166–2012, USA

www.plutobooks.com

British Library Cataloguing in Publication Data
A catalogue record for this book is available from the British Library

Library of Congress Cataloging in Publication Data
applied for

ISBN 0 7453 1670 0 hardback
ISBN 0 7453 1669 7 paperback

10   09   08   07   06   05   04   03   02   01
10   9   8   7   6   5   4   3   2   1

Designed and produced for Pluto Press by
Chase Publishing Services, Fortescue, Sidmouth EX10 9QG
Typeset from disk by Stanford DTP Services, Northampton
Printed in the European Union by TJ International, Padstow, England

FOR DEE

On the political significance of film...At no point in time, no matter how utopian, will anyone win the masses over to a higher art; they can be won over only to one that is nearer to them. And the difficulty consists precisely in finding a form for art such that, with the best conscience in the world, one could hold that it *is* a higher art. This will never happen with most of what is propagated by the avant-garde of the bourgeoisie.

Walter Benjamin, *The Arcades Project*

Now, political education means opening...minds, awakening them, and allowing the birth of their intelligence; as Cesaire said, it is 'to invent souls'. To educate the masses politically does not mean, cannot mean, making a political speech. What it means is to try, relentlessly and passionately, to teach the masses that everything depends on them.

Frantz Fanon, *The Wretched of the Earth*

Contents

Introduction   1

1 Third Cinema as Critical Practice: A Case Study of
   The Battle of Algiers   5

2 Precursors   25

3 Dialectics of First and Third Cinema   47

4 Dialectics of Second Cinema: The Bandit   82

5 Dialectics of Third Cinema   108

Bibliography   157
Index   161

Acknowledgements

The seed for this book was planted back in the early 1990s when I co-taught Third Cinema with Bob Barker at the University of North London. It was his module that was structured around a passage through First, Second and Third Cinema, a structure which got me thinking along the lines which eventually ended up with the writing of this book. I have been teaching Third Cinema at the West London Institute of Higher Education, subsequently integrated into Brunel University, for a number of years. During that time I learned a lot about Third Cinema, teaching and being taught by some very good students. This book was easy to write as a result and whatever merits it may have derive largely from that classroom experience.

Introduction

All films are political, but films are not all political in the same way. If the first half of this aphorism is true, then the definition of a *political film* extends all the way from Sergei Eisenstein's *Strike* (1924) to *Kevin and Perry Go Large* (2000). The second half of the aphorism, that films are political in different ways, returns us to a more specific sense of what constitutes a political film. All the films discussed in this book are political in the sense that they in one way or another address unequal access to and distribution of material and cultural resources, and the hierarchies of legitimacy and status accorded to those differentials. This book is about developing a film practice and criticism which is best suited to addressing those inequalities and differentials. The most advanced and sophisticated body of political films which the medium has produced to date is Third Cinema. This cinema, which emerged in the 1960s and 1970s, moved onto the film studies curriculum in the 1980s, placed there largely by Teshome Gabriel's groundbreaking book *Third Cinema in the Third World*. The title is significant because Third Cinema emerged primarily in the Third World and has since been frequently conflated with Third World Cinema (another category in its own right). For Third Cinema, as Gabriel insisted, is not a cinema defined by geography; it is a cinema primarily defined by its socialist politics.

What counts as political is indeed a political question of course. The bourgeois separation of politics and economics, representation and commerce, is far from innocent, while the spread of the political into the personal and the cultural was a major aim and achievement of feminism. Third Cinema is a political cinema about much more than politics in the narrow sense. It is a cinema of social and cultural emancipation and one of the arguments of this book is that such emancipations cannot be achieved merely in the political realm of the state. Social and cultural emancipation needs a much more fundamental and pervasive transformation, and if cinema is to make its own, relatively modest contribution, it too must feel the heat of such transformations, not only as films, but in its modes of production and reception. Third Cinema is such a cinema, or at least it is as close as we can get to such a cinema *this* side of such profound transformations.

1

Yet in 1996, at a BFI-sponsored conference on African cinema, the British filmmaker John Akomfrah declared Third Cinema to be dead. There was no dissent from the audience. This book aims to refute that claim. In order to do that however, Third Cinema has to be developed as a theory, as a *critical* practice which is inspired by and tries to be adequate to Third Cinema films. But not only them. One of the curious deficiencies of Third Cinema theory has been its underdevelopment *vis-à-vis* First Cinema (dominant, mainstream) and Second Cinema (art, authorial). To develop Third Cinema *theory* is to try and illuminate its relations with and what is at stake in the differences between First, Second and Third Cinema. So terms need to be clarified and their relations and differences with each other explored.

Chapter One works as an introduction to defining Third Cinema while also developing Third Cinema as a critical practice. I focus here on Gillo Pontecorvo's classic film of national liberation, *The Battle of Algiers* (1965). I argue that the film lies at the intersection of Cinemas One, Two and Three, affording us the opportunity to discuss all three categories. Developing Third Cinema as a critical practice means pinpointing quite precisely at the level of textual analysis the interactions of First, Second and Third Cinema strategies within the film. Exploring its critical reception and its selective appropriation of ideas from Fanon, I will argue that the film ultimately fails to *transform* its First and Second cinema components into the service of Third Cinema. In this way we can assess what is at stake, politically, in such a judgement.

In Chapter Two I look at the important European precursors to Third Cinema, indicating the relevance of the work of Eisenstein, Vertov, Lukács, Brecht and Benjamin and tracing the continuities and differences between them and Third Cinema. Just as Third Cinema emerged in the context of revolutionary struggles, the work of these critics and cultural producers was crucially informed by the revolutionary turbulence between 1917 and the late 1930s. Unsurprisingly, their work prefigures key issues for the Third Cineastes: questions around realism, around cultural transformations and their relationship to social change, around the avant-garde and its relationship to the masses and around the political implications of using cinematic strategies in a particular way, were all to return once more, in new contexts and with new inflections, in the 1960s.

Chapter Three juxtaposes First and Third Cinema to further define the latter through a critique of the former at both the level of production practices and textual strategies. As a mode of production,

Third Cinema has pioneered collective and democratic working practices. In particular, it has sought to foster the participation of the people who constitute the subject matter of the films. The chapter also explores the constraints within which Third Cinema works, squeezed as it is between monopoly capital which dominates production, distribution and exhibition, and/or state interference. In extreme instances of danger or crisis, Third Cinema, as we shall see, has pioneered 'guerrilla filmmaking'.

At the textual level, I explore the importance of being able to represent history as an open-ended site of conflict and change and compare Spielberg's *Amistad* (1997) with Alea's *The Last Supper* (1976) and Sembene's *Camp de Thiaroye* (1987). This chapter also explores the importance of political commitment for Third Cinema, which rejects any aspiration to be 'objective', that is, neutral. Because Third Cinema is politically committed, it is also a cinema crucially interested in the processes by which people become politicised. The two go hand in hand. Here I compare Costa Gavras's *Missing* (1981) with Patricio Guzman's *The Battle of Chile* (1973–6). The dialectics of First and Third Cinema are such that while they often converge on similar material (history, the coup in Chile) they diverge in their treatments of that material. There is also a dialectic going on at the level of aesthetic strategies. We shall see many instances in this book of Third Cinema appropriating First Cinema strategies for its own use. But the dialectics work both ways. I explore how a First Cinema film, *Indochine* (1991), appropriates the crucial concept of popular memory for its own purposes.

Chapter Four explores the dialectics between Second Cinema and Third Cinema via the cinematic figure of the bandit. Drawing on the work of Eric Hobsbawm on banditry, I suggest that the significance of the bandit resides in what he, or (occasionally) she, tells us about the social structure being depicted. Herein lies the secret of the bandit as popular hero, both historically and as they are recycled in mass popular culture. It is crucial in defining the cinematic bandit to distinguish them from the gangster. I explore three films in detail: the Turkish set *Eskiya* (1997), the Indian set *Bandit Queen* (1994) and the Irish-set *The General* (1998). While a vehicle for social critique, the bandit's struggle (an *ur*-figure for the guerrilla fighter) is essentially defensive, isolated, individualistic and lacks the leverage required for social transformation.

The final chapter explores the temporal dialectics between Third Cinema in its original historical moment of emergence (the 1960s) and its contemporary manifestations. Using Walter Benjamin's image of the Angel of History, I explore the political urgency of memory. Popular memory is an important resource for Third Cinema, but a *memory of* Third Cinema, as opposed to simply pronouncing it 'dead', is also required. This leads me on to a brief critique of postcolonial theory, the obvious alternative and contesting perspective on themes and concerns associated with Third Cinema. In rescuing Third Cinema from what E. P. Thompson called the condescension of posterity, I give a detailed analysis of Solanas and Getino's manifesto 'Towards a Third Cinema'. I situate it in its national and historical context to understand its strength and limitations. I then explore contemporary examples of Third Cinema that have shifted to the use of allegory and satire as well as enacting transformations of popular genres such as the musical. I return to the theoretical development of Third Cinema with a consideration of Tomás Gutiérrez Alea's significant essay 'The Viewer's Dialectic', before drawing together some of the themes and issues around Third Cinema in general and Alea's essay in particular in a discussion of Juan Carlos Tabio's *The Elephant and the Bicycle* (1995).

On all the social indices (measurements of poverty, longevity, pollution, diet, access to technology, culture, medicine and so forth) it is clear that there are fundamental divisions of wealth and opportunity within nations and regions and between nations and regions. A government programme here, some aid there, operates very much at the margins of this situation which in all its fundamentals, stays static, or more accurately, gets worse. It would be a modest contribution to changing consciousness and raising awareness if we had a film practice that can be adequate to addressing the crisis. Similarly, if we had a film criticism adequate to both the crisis and a radical film practice.

1 Third Cinema as Critical Practice: A Case Study of *The Battle of Algiers*

What is Third Cinema? Above all the term designates a body of theory and filmmaking practice committed to social and cultural emancipation. This body of filmmaking is small, indeed tiny in terms of world cinema output. Yet Third Cinema films are amongst the most exciting and challenging films ever to be made, their political and cultural significance amplified by their proximity and intervention into the major historical processes of the epoch. Third Cinema can work with different forms of documentary and across the range of fictional genres. It challenges both the way cinema is conventionally made (for example, it has pioneered collective and democratic production methods) and the way it is consumed. It refuses to be mere entertainment, yet banish from your mind a cinema that is worthy but dull or a cinema of simplistic polemics. Third Cinema is passionate, angry, often satirical, always complex. Yet at the level of theory, Third Cinema is a concept in need of development in the face of its underdevelopment; a concept in need of clarification in the face of confusion and misunderstanding; a concept in need of defence in the face of contesting and indeed hostile theories and politics. Although it has precursors, particularly in the Soviet cinema of the 1920s, it emerged in the decade after and was influenced by the 1959 Cuban Revolution.

From the beginning, Third Cinema, like revolutionary praxis generally, sought to integrate theory and practice – key filmmakers, particularly, but not exclusively the Latin Americans, also wrote manifestos and considered theoretical reflections on the cultural and political implications of filmmaking. The Brazilian filmmaker Glauber Rocha, founder member of that country's Cinema Novo in the 1960s, spoke of a 'cinema of hunger', one desperate for social and cultural justice (Rocha, 1997:59–61). Julio Garciá Espinosa, the Cuban filmmaker and one-time director of the Cuban Film Institute, rejected the technical and aesthetic criteria of dominant cinema, advocating instead an 'imperfect cinema' (Espinosa, 1997:71–82). Fernando Birri, the Argentinian filmmaker who revolutionised documentary filmmaking in that country, called for a cinema that awakens/clarifies and strengthens a revolutionary consciousness; a cinema that disturbs, shocks and weakens reactionary ideas; a cinema that is anti-bourgeois at a national level and anti-imperialist at an international level; and a cinema that intervenes in the process of creating new people, new societies, new histories, new art and new cinemas (Birri, 1997a:86–7). But it was the Argentinian filmmakers Solanas and Getino (1997:33–58) who coined the term 'Third Cinema' in their theoretical reflections on their groundbreaking documentary *The Hour of the Furnaces* (1968).

However, although theory was always a key component of Third Cinema, as a body of theoretical work, it remains significantly underdeveloped in terms of its grasp of First Cinema and Second Cinema. Understandably, the main concern, not only in the 1960s/early 1970s, but in the 'second wave' of interest in Third Cinema during the 1980s (see Gabriel, 1982 and Pines and Willemen, 1989), has been to develop theory in a way that is immediately and directly relevant to Third Cinema filmmaking. First and Second Cinema was sketched by Getino and Solanas as, respectively, dominant commercial cinema and art cinema (1997:33–4). And that has remained pretty much that within Third Cinema theory. There are four reasons why this is no longer satisfactory and why Third Cinema, if it is to develop theoretically, that is as a critical practice, must develop its understanding of First and Second Cinema.

1) We need more nuanced and complex accounts of First and Second Cinema in order to rescue Third Cinema from the common conflation that is made between Third Cinema and Third World Cinema. Third Cinema is *not* to be restricted to the so-called Third World. First, Second and Third Cinemas do not designate geographical areas, but institutional structures/working practices, associated aesthetic strategies and their attendant cultural politics. Thus, if we understand First and Second Cinema in more complexity, we will be more ready to understand that we can have First and Second Cinema in the Third World and Third Cinema in the First World.

2) Since First, Second and Third Cinemas denote institutional practices and sets of aesthetic strategies, it follows that all three cinemas take up their own distinctive *positionings* in relation to a shared referent: i.e. the historical, social world around them. Thus each cinema also has relations of dialogue, interchange and transformation between them as each works over and on the same

cultural/political material (e.g. anticolonial struggle), but pulls and shapes the material into different, often radically different, meanings and possibilities. From the beginning, Third Cinema was understood, by Birri for example, as a dialectical transformation of First and Second Cinema, not a simple rejection of them.

> 'Commercial' cinema has won its audience by any method going. We cannot support it. The 'cinema of expression' uses the best methods, and scorns the mass audience. We cannot support it either. Once again, the contradiction between art and industry is resolved very badly, except for the 'select' minority who make up the audience of the 'cinema of expression', for whom such a solution is perfectly satisfactory. (Birri, 1997a:88)

But we cannot understand this dialectical transformation – what Third Cinema is/could be, what it has to offer that the other cinemas do not, why it is so urgently needed and the complex relations of interchange and difference between First, Second and Third Cinema – if we have only a rudimentary grasp of Cinemas One and Two.

3) Extending Third Cinema into the analysis of First and Second Cinema should also be seen as a counter-hegemonic move aimed at challenging some of the more ivory-towered paradigms within film studies, particularly Lacanian psychoanalysis, postcolonial studies and postmodernism. Surveying these theoretical currents, one is reminded of the opening pages of *The German Ideology*, where Marx and Engels ridicule German academics and intellectuals who imagine that the 'general chaos' and 'universal ferment' of ideas generated by the demise of Hegelian philosophy has produced a 'revolution beside which the French Revolution was child's play' (1989:39). Their location within the social division of labour makes intellectuals peculiarly prone to over-estimating the power of ideas and underestimating the importance of the social forces which make or break ideas. Postmodernism, for example, advocates a liberal multiculturalism or hybridity at the expense of understanding the material divisions that can exist irrespective of cultural exchanges, or how the struggle for resources which have been made scarce due to the social relations of production unleashes (as it did in formerly cosmopolitian Sarajevo) the fundamentalist cultural politics (nationalism and ethnic tribalism) against which advocacy of liberal hybridity is a mere straw in the wind. It would be peculiar, in a book about cinema, to dismiss the importance of ideas, but the power, direction and meaning of ideas depends on the social forces with which they are articulated. A Third Cinema analysis of Cinemas One, Two and Three helps lay the basis for a genuinely socialist, indeed, Marxist engagement with the medium and broaden the concerns of film studies beyond the rather narrow middle-class constituency which currently limits it.

4) Finally, developing the theory of Third Cinema may be seen as something of a 'holding operation' in the dark times of neo-liberalism's hegemony. Revolutionary conjunctures are the womb from which Third Cinema emerges, and while Third Cinema can be made in conditions which are temporally and spatially distant from revolutionary conjunctures (examples of Third Cinema are still being made today), inspiration, political tradition and memory are the umbilical cord that nourishes Third Cinema in a time of reaction and barbarism. When the time comes, as it surely must (the very survival of the human race depends upon it), for new revolutionary upheavals, then any interim developments in the theory of Third Cinema may make a small contribution to subsequent practical interventions.

ONCE AGAIN, *THE BATTLE OF ALGIERS*

If we can find a single film that straddles First, Second and Third Cinemas, while nevertheless operating largely within the gravitational pull of First and Second Cinema, then we are in a better position to understand the complex cultural interactions designated by these numerical categories, as well as the theoretical and political issues at stake in making distinctions between these cinemas. Gillo Pontecorvo's 1965 film *The Battle of Algiers*, much written about, and enjoying the status of a 'classic', will serve as one such text. As an Italian communist and anti-fascist, Pontecorvo had fought against Italian fascism and the subsequent German occupation of Italy during the Second World War. *The Battle of Algiers* was made in Algeria with the blessing and help of the Algerian government in 1965, three years after independence had been won from France. So, clearly the film was made in conditions that allowed it proximity to the social, historical and cultural specificities of the Algerian people, while the film's key cultural worker, the director, had some first-hand knowledge and experience of the kind of guerrilla warfare that the Algerian National Liberation Front (FLN) deployed. Although

Robert Stam and Louise Spence describe *The Battle of Algiers* as a 'Third World' film (1985), the key creative positions in the production of the film were occupied by Italians. Pontecorvo also co-wrote the script with Franco Solinas and collaborated with Ennio Morricone on the music track. It makes more sense then to locate *The Battle of Algiers* as a European film about the Third World. This does *not* of course determine its location within our three categories of cinema. Conversely, if the film were more authentically Algerian, it would not automatically qualify as Third Cinema, since (it is worth restating) Third Cinema and Third World Cinema are *not* the same thing. Is geography irrelevant then? Not quite. Locating *The Battle of Algiers* geographically as European does give us some indication of the cultural influences on the film. From the perspective of Third Cinema, the task of the filmmaker is to be adequately cognisant of the politics of those cultural influences and be ready, if necessary, to rework them.

THE BATTLE OF ALGIERS: THE CRITICAL RECEPTION

The critical reception of the film has always in fact been mixed. At the time of its release it won a number of prestigious awards on the international film festival circuit, but it was also criticised by writers and filmmakers on the left for being too similar to dominant cinema and not sufficiently reworking the language of the medium. Peter Sainsbury for example complained that the film mobilised the thriller format in its depiction of a 'suspenseful battle of tactics between hunters and hunted, action and counter-action' which blocked exploration of the political complexities and processes of the Algerian revolution (1971:6). As we shall see, this critique is made with some justification. Nevertheless, one can also sympathise with Pontecorvo when he rejects what he calls the bourgeois 'rich kids' who, in advocating radical avant-garde aesthetic strategies, dismiss his film (and it is a great film in many ways) as hopelessly compromised by its attachment to dramatic action, narrative, character identification and so on. From this avant-garde position, articulated for example by the French journal *Cahiers du cinéma*, Pontecorvo's film exists wholly 'within the system'.

Pontecorvo's critics wanted filmmakers to engage much more radically with questions of form, with the language of cinema, its aesthetic strategies, its signifying practices and interrogate the politics of those formal operations (Harvey, 1980:62). These are all perfectly legitimate and indeed urgent questions, and a vital component of Third Cinema. However, the persistent failure of the western avant-garde is its tendency to move from a self-conscious exploration of form for the purpose of 'social intelligibility' to a celebration of form for its own sake. (The phrase 'social intelligibility' refers to the ambition to make the social world intelligible or explicable. It yokes the question of artistic form to cognition and knowledge. The phrase comes from Paul Willemen's excellent essay on Third Cinema (1989).) The celebration of form for its own sake (known as formalism) eclipses the substantive 'content' of a cultural artifact, while aesthetic matters generally are severed from the political, social and economic circumstances in which the cultural artifact circulates. The tension between a necessary attention to form and the dangerous lure of formalism can be traced back to Trotsky's debate with the Russian avant-garde in the 1920s, and it drove much radical film theory and practice in the 1970s into something of an élitist cul-de-sac (Harvey, 1980:108–10).

The great advantage of Third Cinema is that while it is politically oppositional to dominant cinema (and Second Cinema), it does not seek, at the level of form and cinematic language, to reinvent cinema from scratch (it is too interested in history for that); nor does it adopt a position of pure opposition on the question of form (it is too interested in communication for that); instead, its relation to First and Second Cinema is dialectical: i.e. it seeks to *transform* rather than simply reject these cinemas; it seeks to bring out their stifled potentialities, those aspects of the social world they repress or only obliquely acknowledge; Third Cinema seeks to detach what is positive, life-affirming and critical from Cinemas One and Two and give them a more expanded, socially connected articulation.

Pontecorvo's response to his critics correctly identified two blindspots within formalism. Firstly, he argued that 'the system', capitalism, is *contradictory*, something that is evident to any cultural theory and practice which has not withdrawn from a wider world of political and social conflict.

I believe that a producer will make a political film, even if it is against his class sense, as long as he thinks he can make money with it. I think he would even make a film which shows that his father is a thief and his mother a whore if he is sure to make money. So it depends on the situation at the moment. (Georgakas and Rubenstein, 1983:95)

Here Pontecorvo identifies a contradiction between the short-term interests of capitalism (to make money) and its long-term interests (not to produce ideas that may challenge its legitimacy). This contradiction opens an important institutional and cultural space 'within the system' for progressive filmmaking such as Pontecorvo's and, even closer to dominant cinema, films like Costa Gavras's *Missing* (1981) and John Boorman's *The Emerald Forest* (1985). However, Pontecorvo's point notwithstanding, it is still legitimate to ask what the limits of such films are: what meanings can they not articulate? what ambitions can they not countenance? It is a crucial component of Third Cinema to expand our political and cultural horizons, to imagine alternatives to what is and refuse to accept what is as coterminous with what can be. This expansion of our horizons is as much about what cinema can and cannot do as it is about calling for change in the wider social world. So while there are contradictions within capitalism, while there is some latitude for progressive cultural workers, we must not block up our capacity to imagine radically different cinemas and visions of radically different social and political relations. In this sense Third Cinema is a utopian cinema, anticipating radical change, harbouring its potential in the present and remembering where it has flowered in the past.

Pontecorvo's second argument in defence of his film also has its merits but, again, there are caveats which have to be entered. Pontecorvo points out that for those people actively involved in revolutionary politics (the Cubans, the Black Panthers, etc.) the film has been received more positively. Pontecorvo's claims for his film are modest. It may not be 'a great help but a help' (Georgakas and Rubenstein, 1983:95) to such groups involved in struggles against racism and imperialism. Certainly Pontecorvo is right to point to the role of the audience, that they are social beings located in particular times and places, potentially very active in engaging with the cinematic text. It is precisely this question of the role of the audience and the nature of their engagement with the text that is central to Third Cinema. Indeed Third Cinema has appropriated the theme of the active spectator from the avant-garde. As Espinosa noted in an early Third Cinema manifesto:

There's a widespread tendency in modern art to make the spectator participate ever more fully. If he [*sic*] participates to a greater and greater degree, where will the process end up? Isn't the logical outcome – or shouldn't it in fact be – that he will cease being a spectator altogether? This simultaneously represents a tendency towards collectivism and toward individualism. Once we admit the possibility of universal participation, aren't we also admitting the individual creative potential which we all have? (Espinosa, 1997:77)

The transformation that Third Cinema effects on the modern art/active spectator relationship is to relocate them both back into the broader social struggles from which they have been severed, so that the active spectator is no longer engaged in a purely aesthetic activity. It is this broader social context which Pontecorvo is gesturing to.

Nevertheless, if we are interested in the *relationship* between text and audience, we must still ask what the text contributes to the production of meaning. And here *The Battle of Algiers* may be found wanting. Veronica Horwell opens her review of the film after another re-release with these words: 'I know an Army officer who screened a video of *The Battle of Algiers* to his lads in Northern Ireland almost as a training film; I've been told his opposite numbers did the same' (Horwell, 1997:9).

If the British officer could show the film to his rank and file without apparently worrying that they may as a result start to question why they happen to be an occupying force in another country, then that could, from a Third Cinema perspective, indicate an unhelpful ambiguity or loss of analytical power. However, it is precisely the fact that the film could be shown to both sides in the conflict which many critics would take to be a sign of the film's greatest strength. The *Monthly Film Bulletin* describes the film's 'extraordinary fairmindedness'(Dawson, 1971:68) while *Time Out* praised the film's 'scrupulous balance' (Time Out, 1998:60).

This appeal to objectivity is a theme within the critical reception of Second Cinema and is symptomatic of this Cinema's base in the middle class. The claim to see 'both sides' corresponds remarkably closely to their social position, caught as they are between capital and labour. The *Time Out* review of Mira Nair's *Salaam Bombay!* (1988), about children begging on the streets of the Indian city, notes that 'the film brings the lives of all its characters into a common embrace, never pointing a finger of blame but constantly emphasising the difficulties and dangers that surround young and old alike' (Time Out, 1998:751). Heaven help us that a film should actually identify those responsible for such poverty! Third Cinema however would want to point the finger, it would want, in Espinosa's words, to *'show the process which generates the problems'* (1997:81, my emphasis). But to do that requires taking a position, making a commitment. Thus Third Cinema has an entirely different epistemological foundation to Second Cinema and the critical discourse which frames and interprets such films. For the latter, knowledge about the world is generated at a higher level by *not* unequivocally committing to a position or cause. Lurking behind the critics' valorisation of 'balance', 'objectivity', 'distance' and other such terms, lies an old distinction between art and politics or art and propaganda. Third Cinema deconstructs this binary because it is characterised by unequivocal commitment to a position or cause but does not see itself as 'propaganda'. Commitment to a cause, even unequivocal commitment, is not the same as suspending your critical faculties; it is not the same as dogma. Espinosa again: 'A new poetics for cinema will, above all, be a "partisan" and "committed" poetics, a "committed" art, a consciously and resolutely "committed" cinema – that is to say, an "imperfect" cinema. An "impartial" or "uncommitted" one, as a complete aesthetic activity, will only be possible when it is the people who make art' (1997:79).

In this rather tortuous passage Espinosa is arguing that an 'impartial' art is premature in a world full of 'partialities' (social, economic and cultural inequalities). Only when these imperfections have been addressed can art, in good faith, be considered 'uncommitted'. When it is the people who make art, art will no longer be caught up in sectional interests. This last utopian image requires a projection forward into an almost unimaginably transformed future. The key point though is that we do not live in such a world today and so art cannot be divorced from the conflictual social interests which are at play.

With the decline of the political avant-garde in the west, the critical reception to *The Battle of Algiers* has become rather uncritical. Re-released in the UK in 1997, Derek Malcolm could describe it as 'the best depiction of a struggle for independence ever made' (1997:9). It must be comforting for the liberal intelligentsia to know that while they are part of a European culture that imposed the most ruthless forms of exploitation on millions of people around the world, it is a culture which can nevertheless produce the best film about the struggles of just some of those millions to liberate themselves from European colonial rule. Except of course *The Battle of Algiers* is not the best depiction ever and only Eurocentric arrogance coupled with ignorance of other cinemas could suggest that it is. And yet even Edward Said, who should know better, having written at length on how the west has framed and constructed the rest of the world, claimed in a *Rear Window* television programme on Pontecorvo, entitled 'The Dictatorship of Truth', that the film was 'unmatched' in its depiction of an anti-colonial struggle. To properly assess the place of *The Battle of Algiers* in the history of radical film requires some 'critical commitment' at the level of critical discourse: that is to say, acknowledging at one and the same time that many of the film's compelling qualities, such as its version of 'realism', are also precisely the sign of its truncated analytical and cognitive power.

THE BATTLE OF ALGIERS: FIRST, SECOND AND THIRD CINEMA

So let us turn to a more detailed analysis of *The Battle of Algiers* in order to delineate how it occupies a contradictory political and aesthetic space. It is a compromised textual formation, never quite managing to *transform* its First and Second Cinema elements and influences fully into the service of Third Cinema, even though it has one foot in the latter category. We are now in a position to identify four key markers that distinguish Third Cinema and through which I want to discuss *The Battle of Algiers*. They are historicity, politicisation, critical commitment and cultural specificity.

Historicity

Third Cinema seeks to develop the means for grasping history as process, change, contradiction and conflict: in short the dialectics of history. History is the great explainer: why we are, where we are and who we are. Willemen quotes Benjamin who saw as his task the need to develop 'the image-creating medium within us to see dimensionally, stereoscopically, into the depth of the historical shade' (1989:11). In *The Battle of Algiers* it is precisely the historical shading that has been erased from the *mise-en-scène*, from the characters and the narrative generally.

At the film's conclusion, after the French paratroopers have eliminated the last FLN cell, a soldier says that 'we've lived in peace with these people for 130 years, there's no reason why we cannot do so again.' The historical record shows that this statement, unchallenged within the film, is demonstrably untrue. The French first invaded Algeria in 1830. Towards the end of the nineteenth century they began to implement settler colonisation, taking over vast tracts of agricultural land and orienting exports to suit the needs of French capitalism. For more than 130 years the Algerians sporadically organised resistance to French control only to see that resistance brutally crushed. In 1945 celebrations of the Allied victory turned into demonstrations for Algerian independence. The French slaughtered an estimated 45,000 at Setif alone (Fanon, 1990:62). The film however does not have the historical memory to recall even this date and event. Instead it charts the first years of military conflict between the FLN and the French police and army (1954–57). How much better it would have been, a student of mine once suggested, if the film had started with the celebrations of 1945 before cutting to 1954. The massacre at Setif would not even have to be alluded to (if French sensibilities are that important): the contradiction between the liberation of France from Nazi domination in the name of democracy and freedom and the continued domination of the colonies would still be sharply revealed. Such sensitivity to the contradictions between European Enlightenment traditions and the grubby material imperatives of European capitalism is the central historical image of a film like Ousmane Sembene's *Camp de Thiaroye* (1987).

It is not that the film offers no articulation of historicity. Take for example the scene of Ali-la-Pointe's arrest in his initial incarnation as a street hustler. Here the soundtrack adopts an asynchronic relationship with the image track. As he is led away, a French voice reads out his details (date of birth, the fact that he is illiterate) and his record as a petty criminal stretching back to juvenile correctional institutions. The voice inhabits the space-time of the latest court through which the just arrested Ali is to pass. At a formal level, it is a wonderfully economic strategy, providing a logical transition to the next scene of Ali in prison, while also briefly sketching in Ali's back-story, where we glimpse what life is like for the ill-educated and poor Algerians under French colonial rule. The problem is that this is all too rare a moment in revealing the historical determinations on the present.

Politicisation

For Third Cinema, one of the key areas of concern which needs to be explored is the process whereby people who have been oppressed and exploited become conscious of that condition and determine to do something about it. For Birri, a revolutionary cinema is one that, above all, seeks to awaken a politicised consciousness in the spectator. Since there is no automatic radical response to the experience of being told in countless ways that you are inferior – and indeed, the most likely outcome is not revolutionary consciousness, but a secret and deep-seated self-loathing – one of the key challenges which *The Battle of Algiers* fails to offer an adequately complex engagement with is how Ali, a petty criminal and illiterate, is transformed into a fighter for national liberation. Whereas *Camp de Thiaroye* devotes the entire film to charting the process whereby African soldiers fighting for France and its colonies during the Second World War come to revolt against their masters, *The Battle of Algiers* deals with this vital question with incredible compression and ellipsis. Ali's conversion to the cause takes place in prison after his arrest. Ali is being held in a cell with other prisoners, but we do not see him engaging in dialogue with the others. Then comes the key moment: Ali's political baptism. A FLN prisoner is being led through the prison to his execution. He shouts, 'Long live Algeria' and the call is taken up by other prisoners in their cells. We cut back to Ali, who now seems suddenly energised: a revelation has struck him. He leaps to the window overlooking the outside courtyard where the condemned man is now being led to the guillotine. The film cuts to several shots of the prison walls and cell windows (but we see no individuals); we hear the guillotine come down and immediately cut to a zoom close-up on Ali's watching face. The experience is almost like a religious epiphany. Ali sees a vision (of a brave man dying for a cause) and is converted. This is underlined by the ellipsis that now omits the rest of his time in prison: the next scene takes place five months later and Ali is getting his first instructions from the FLN. This is a highly individualised presentation of the process of politicisation. There is no suggestion of any interaction with political activists, no learning, no asking questions, just instant revelation.

The way in which the process of politicisation is elided is also reproduced in the film's coda. With the destruction of the FLN in 1957, the film jumps to 1960, when mass demonstrations broke out in Algiers against colonial rule. But our point of entry into the

beginning of the uprising is from the uncomprehending French journalists whose voice-over tells us how unexpected this surge of protest
is; how mysterious after a period of calm. The spectator is positioned
on the outside of the revolution, looking in from the point of view
of the bewildered Europeans.

Critical commitment

We have already seen that the film was valorised by liberal critics for
its fairness to both sides. The film's aspiration towards objectivity
has its roots in Pontecorvo's own national (Second) cinema: the
Italian neorealist movement of the late 1940s and early 1950s. Styl-
istically, *The Battle of Algiers* is firmly rooted in a 1960s reportage:
handheld cameia, grainy black and white stock, zoom lens, long
lenses; while at the level of narrative the flashback structuie would
have been too elaborate for the neorealists, who preferred simple
linear stories, unobtrusive editing and camerawork (Marcus,
1986:22). However, the *goal* of neorealism, to reveal the world with
minimal authorial comment, does manifest itself in the film's low-
key commitment. It is precisely this low-key quality which liberal
critics appear to be praising, because in fact most recognise that the
film is not 'objective' but basically sympathetic to the Algerian cause.
So, there is 'commitment' on the part of the film (and Pontecorvo
denies being 'impartial' on the question of independence) but it is
just not very overt. The problem is that this low-key commitment is
also a sign of a lack in the film's analytical and critical power.

  This can be illustrated via Stam and Spence's discussion of the
film. They praised the way the film subverts the typical focalisation
of First Cinema. They note how the trope of encirclement in the
western genre, where the spectator is located inside the 'besieged
wagon train or fort', helps suture the spectator 'into a colonialist perspective', looking down the barrel of a gun and watching the
American Indian fall from his horse as another settler's bullet finds
its mark (Stam and Spence, 1985:641). By contrast, *The Battle of
Algiers* inverts this spectator identification, locating the viewer with
the 'colonized who are encircled and menaced and with whom we
identify' (Stam and Spence, 1985:642). So the language of First
Cinema (Stam and Spence eschew these terms) has undergone some
reworking; but if it has been filled with a new content, the form and
modes of spectator engagement which they activate have not been
sufficiently reworked. Stam and Spence themselves make the point,

although without drawing out the implications. Discussing the scene where the Algerian women, dressed as Europeans, plant bombs in the European district, Stam and Spence note how spectator positioning, 'makes us want the women to complete their task, not necessarily out of political sympathy but through the mechanism of cinematic identification' (1985:642). This then is a spectatorship that is not being asked to be conscious of the politics of identification; it is an identification made largely at the level of the emotions. And yet one of the key aims of Third Cinema is to seek to bring cognitive and intellectual powers of the spectator into play. As Willemen reminds us, 'the culture industry has become extremely adept at orchestrating emotionality while deliberately atrophying the desire for understanding' (1989:13).

There is something of a Second Cinema reworking of the war film/thriller genre in *The Battle of Algiers*. The relentless emphasis on the military/tactical struggle strips away any room for character development, idiosyncrasies, romance or moments of personal intimacy which First Cinema would be tempted to write in. (The cultural code that Second Cinema is drawing on here is a certain kind of minimalism, evident in Bresson's *A Man Escaped* (1956), for example.) The war dominates the lives of the characters so totally that nothing else can come into the field of representation. Unfortunately, the focus on the military/tactical struggle to the exclusion of all else also blocks the film off from engaging, at least with any complexity, in the politics of revolutionary struggle.

The Cuban film by Sarah Gomez, *One Way or Another* (1977) would be a good example of a text that takes up a position within its socio-historical context, of critical commitment. There is never any doubt that the film is committed to the aims and ideals of the Cuban revolution, while at the same time, it takes up a critical stance insofar as the film explores the *persistence* of class and gender conflicts within Cuba. It is this mode of intervention which means that the film is neither cheerleading propaganda nor does it pretend to be a disinterested objective observer. To return to *The Battle of Algiers*, the key figure articulating the Algerian/African politics of revolutionary commitment was Frantz Fanon.

Fanon was born in Martinique, which had been a French colony since the seventeenth century. He was educated in Paris where he studied medicine and became a psychiatrist. It was here that Fanon started to realise that even though he had been through the French educational system and had proved his intellectual worth, he would never be accepted as an equal. He felt he had been wearing a white mask concealing his black skin. His book *Black Skin/White Mask* was published when he was just 27 years old. In response to metropolitan racism, Fanon requested a post in the colonies and was assigned to a hospital in Algeria in 1954. It was a momentous year, as Fanon was later to record. 'The great victory of the Vietnamese people at Dien Bien Phu is no longer, strictly speaking, a Vietnamese victory. Since July 1954, the question which the colonized peoples have asked themselves has been, "What must be done to bring about another Dien Bien Phu?"' (1990:55).

Having lost North Vietnam, the French were determined not to lose Algeria. As the war there intensified, Fanon's clinic swelled with patients, both French and Algerian. The evident link between mental health and social context led Fanon to conclude that in order to cure patients society had to change. He resigned from the clinic and joined the FLN. His book *The Wretched of the Earth* was published in 1961, the same year he died of leukemia.

The Battle of Algiers has clearly been influenced by *some* of Fanon's political philosophy but, I would suggest, only those elements that could be most easily integrated into the language of First and Second Cinema, thus excluding some of Fanon's more acute and radical ideas. The key Fanonian motif in the film is the all-pervasive role of violence within the colonial set-up. Fanon scandalised the European intelligentsia by reminding them that violence is built into the colonial process whereby one country expropriates the resources of another and subordinates its people. Inevitably, Fanon argued, violence will be a component of the native's struggle to end the violence of colonialism. It was this 'logic' which Pontecorvo has said he wanted to get inside of and explore. There is a very Fanonian moment early on in the film. Ali is being chased by the police just before his arrest. He is tripped up by a French youth. Instead of trying to escape, Ali gets up and head-butts the smiling young man. In that moment, Ali passes through a psychological barrier and demonstrates that he is a fighter. As Fanon puts it: 'At the level of individuals, violence is a cleansing force. It frees the native from his inferiority complex and from his despair and inaction; it makes him fearless and restores his self respect' (1990:74).

There are other Fanonian motifs, such as the image of the colonised city, divided into 'two zones' of 'reciprocal exclusivity', a 'world cut in two...inhabited by two different species' (Fanon, 1990:30). Thus we see the camera pan across the European district –

rich, affluent, wide streets with modern cars – and then onto the Algerian casbah – old, poor, its buildings crumbling, its streets narrow and squalid.

Then there is the figure of Ali himself, who corresponds to the *lumpen-proletariat*, the people who have nothing, no stake within the colonial system, who are most likely, Fanon contended, to be at the forefront of the liberation struggle. Faith in people to transform themselves and their lives is a prerequisite for any revolutionary. But it can be a thin line between faith and romanticism. Fanon's singling out of the 'pimps, the hooligans, the unemployed and the petty criminals' (1990:103) as heroes of the struggle can be described as romantic because it is their outsider status, their marginality to the social order which is seen as guaranteeing their authentic revolutionary capacity. It is a romanticism that the film itself shares. While the Algerian people as a collective force are evident within the film, this mass protagonist is counter-balanced by the centrality of Ali. The film begins in 1957: his is the last FLN cell to be destroyed by the French military. A flashback then takes us to 1954 and to Ali as a street hustler. At the end of the film, we arrive back at Ali's imminent destruction. Along the way, we have seen Ali's commander, Djafar, give himself up rather than die a pointless death. Ali's scene, however, brings out the Algerian people on the rooftops, watching and waiting for the moment when his little hideaway is blown to pieces. The problem with focalising much (although not all) of the story through Ali, coupled with the presentation of his conversion to the cause and the excessive focus on the military/tactical battle, is that he becomes simply the 'hardman' familiar from First Cinema: that is a thoroughly depoliticised fighter. We never learn what Ali's political convictions were/are and how they have changed, or not, in the course of the struggle.

The more radical elements in Fanon's political philosophy are to be found not in his writing on violence, or his lionisation of the peasantry or the *lumpen-proletariat*, but in his broader critique of the social order. In particular he is clear-eyed about the class differences within the liberation struggle. Exploitation, he suggested, 'can wear a black face, or an Arab one' (1990:116). He constantly warned about the necessity for the liberation leaders, overwhelmingly middle class, to communicate lucidly with the people and not in a professionalised discourse designed to prove that the 'masses have to be managed from above' (1990:152). For Fanon, the difficult task of developing a relationship between the revolutionary party and the people, so that the latter becomes a fully involved participant in the transformation of society, is of crucial importance. Fanon's concern with educating and politicising the people is linked to his warnings concerning what happens after liberation has been achieved: 'we must repeat, it is absolutely necessary to oppose vigorously and definitively the birth of a national bourgeoisie and a privileged caste' (1990:163).

Yet *The Battle of Algiers* does not register the significance of class difference within the liberation struggle. The FLN is presented as a homogeneous unity. The historical significance of these components of Fanon's thought was unfortunately confirmed when a 1965 putsch in Algeria put in place a corrupt military junta. Today, in the wake of the disappointments of a post-apartheid South Africa, Fanon's concern about how the masses are shut out of power by the elites continues to resonate.

Another key issue in the political struggle that the film avoids altogether is that of gender. One of the film's most powerful sequences shows the Algerian women, disguised as Europeans, planting bombs in two cafés and the airport. The role of women in revolutionary struggles, involving themselves in activities, military and political, which customs and traditions around the world have usually reserved exclusively for men, always raises the most profound gender questions. It is inconceivable that the FLN's willingness to use women in the struggle would not have generated, within an Islamic culture, both resistance to and new ideas about female equality. Again, the film fails to register these seismic shifts in gender roles.

It has been argued by Ranjana Khanna that Third Cinema is incapable of engaging with gender politics in a way which calls into question male domination (1988:13–31). Her methodology though is flawed. She uses *The Battle of Algiers* as an example of the limitations of Third Cinema on the issue of gender. But, as I have argued, the film does not belong primarily in that cinematic category and so making it sufficiently representative to stand in for Third Cinema as a whole is untenable (and a peculiarly homogenising strategy for someone so interested in difference). Part of Khanna's problem is that she misconceives what constitutes Second Cinema. While correctly identifying it as a cinema that seeks to engage with the national realities marginalised by the dominant media, she wrongly suggests that Second Cinema 'uses conventional cinematic techniques' (1988:13). Now, this is rather vague, since all techniques use conventions – but in fact Khanna is referring to the dominant cinematic techniques of First Cinema. But historically Second Cinema (as an art cinema) has developed alternative forms of expression to First Cinema. Khanna's example of a Second Cinema film reveals her misconception. She suggests Attenborough's *Gandhi* (1982), presumably because it is about India, when clearly it is primarily (although not exclusively) a First Cinema bio-pic with little rootedness in the national culture it represents. A better example of Indian Second Cinema might be *Bandit Queen* (Shekhar Kapur, 1994). However, the example of *Gandhi* functions strategically in her argument (because there is evidently a difference in kind between *Gandhi* and *The Battle of Algiers*) to help (mis)locate Pontecorvo's film primarily in the Third Cinema category, when the difference between the two films is primarily the difference between First and Second Cinema.

Cultural specificity

Essentially the above categories have been calling for a cinema grounded in the socio-historical processes which it seeks to represent. But a grounding in the cultural dynamics of the milieu deserves a special category because cinema is part of culture and its greatest contribution can be in the realm of culture. Third Cinema is characterised by its intimacy and familiarity with culture – both in the specific sense of cultural production (for example, song, dance, theatre, rituals, cinema, literature) and in the broader sense of the word (the nuances of everyday living). Further, Third Cinema explores how culture is a site of political struggle. History has shown that one of the first things which colonialism and imperialism attempt to control, in parallel with economic resources, is culture, where values and beliefs and identities are forged and re-forged. Yet Third Cinema is not a parochial defence of native or indigenous culture: its attention to class differences and its internationalism helps guard against that. Fanon warned against the uncritical cele-bration of the native's culture as much as he warned against the uncritical assimilation of the culture of the colonialists (1990:166–99). Here Third Cinema anticipates and touches borders with postcolonial theory and its master concept of hybridity. Except postcolonial theory is exactly that, a theory with little practical application generated largely within academia; a discourse which disavows its class roots, since class is virtually absent from its critical vocabulary. Third Cinema by contrast is a theory and a practice; as the latter it has involved intellectuals in concrete political struggles where their lives and liberty have often been at risk. And Third Cinema as a theory and practice has demonstrated a remarkable self-reflexivity about its own class roots; interrogating the intellectual's position *vis-à-vis* both the culture of the imperial metropolis and the masses below them.

The Battle of Algiers displays a considerable understanding around the importance of culture as one front – and an important front – in the wider political struggle for national liberation. Stam and Spence discuss how the European disguise that the Algerian women adopt to pass bombs through the checkpoints turns the colonisers' implicit 'us and them' racism to the native's advantage (1985:643–4). Elsewhere, we see the FLN perform a secret Islamic wedding service while also adapting and shortening it so as to reduce the risks of detection. When, at a checkpoint, a child commandeers a French loudspeaker and urges the Algerians to 'have no fear', the women respond with their distinctive Arab cry. Yet the scene that shows French paratroopers torturing Algerians is cast overwhelmingly in the terms of European sound and imagery. On the image track, the Algerians are tied up, arms outstretched, or hanging upside down on a cross-like structure, heads turned to one side; and on the soundtrack, classical European music with church organs. Together, these signifiers of the crucifixion, the Christian motif of suffering and the religious music, so culturally remote from the story material, de-historicise a specific struggle in time and space, turning a story from the anti-colonial liberation movements into a timeless tragedy, a universal story, a comment on the human condition and other such depoliticising aesthetic concepts.

This chapter has endeavoured to develop First and Second Cinema as categories for a critical practice from a Third Cinema perspective. Using *The Battle of Algiers* as an example, I have argued that a film may draw on ideas, themes and strategies associated with all three cinemas, although it may finally be located as primarily a First, Second or Third Cinema film. The point of such categorisations is to try to track the processes or dialectical relationships by which ideas, themes and strategies shuttle back and forth between these cinemas and change as they do so. If Third Cinema's relations with

First and Second Cinema have been underdeveloped, one area of Third Cinema theory has been much commented on. While Third Cinema emerged in the 1960s, its theories and practices have antecedents, particularly in the work of European Marxists between the World Wars (Burton, 1997 and Willemen, 1989). It is to these precursors that we now need to turn.

2   Precursors

This chapter will explore some aspects of the theories and practices of key cultural thinkers working during the 1920s and 1930s. They are the filmmakers Sergei Eisenstein and Dziga Vertov, the literary critic and philosopher Georg Lukács, the dramatist Bertolt Brecht and the cultural critic and philosopher Walter Benjamin. All were Marxists and each had distinctive positions on the question of the politics of aesthetics. In their work we will find ideas that anticipate some of the concerns and strategies of Third Cinema although, as we shall see, temporal and geographical differences between these Europeans and Third Cinema in Latin America and Africa mean that there are differences as well as continuities to be identified.

Just as Third Cinema is unthinkable without it in some way tapping into the revolutionary struggles of the exploited and the oppressed, so the work of our European thinkers was fundamentally shaped by the revolutionary conjuncture of the inter-war years: 1917–39. Briefly, then, we need to sketch in that historical context.

CRISIS AND REVOLT

Lenin described the First World War as: 'that ocean of blood that has been shed by the ten million killed and twenty million maimed in the great, noble, liberating and holy war to decide whether the British or the German robbers are to get most of the [colonial] spoils, whether the British or the German thugs are to be the *foremost* in throttling the weak nations all over the world' (Lenin, 1978:7).

As the slaughter entered its final stages, two revolutions in Russia erupted in 1917. The first replaced the Czarist monarchy; the second, the October Revolution, displaced the bourgeois government which had taken the Czar's place. For the first time the organised working class had taken the centre stage of history and propelled to power a party (Lenin's Bolsheviks) who claimed to represent (and initially, on balance, did represent) the interests of labour *against* capital. This revolution opened up a period of revolutionary struggles across Europe (and indeed in many of the colonies as well). The response of the propertied classes when seriously challenged by labour was to facilitate the rise of Fascism in Italy, Germany and Spain, so as to break the organisations of labour.

This turning towards Fascism as a response to the claims of labour of course anticipates the situation in Latin America in the post-Second World War period where time and again the ruling classes turn to the military – usually backed by Washington and the CIA, anxious to protect, not freedom and justice, but American capital investments – to crush the socialist hopes and aspirations of workers, peasants and progressive fractions of the intelligentsia. In the late 1980s and 1990s, many of those regimes gave way to some sort of elected representation. But this new democratic politics remains often quite compromised by the threatening presence of the military (Don't step out of line or we will be back!) while politically they subjugate themselves entirely to market capitalism. All this involves, as we shall see in the final chapter, the question of memory and whether one should move on and forget the past in a kind of public mass amnesia, or whether the past needs to be retained as a vital part of identity and as a vital resource for alternatives to the present social order.

Unsurprisingly, Third Cinema takes the latter position and so, recalling our key European figures from a time which may seem very remote and distant is part and parcel of the methodology of the cinema we are exploring. In Europe the rise of Fascism during the 1920s and 1930s rescued capitalism from socialism but it also intensified national rivalries leading to war in 1939. By this time the revolution in Russia and the nations it had corralled into the Soviet Union had failed. Genuine revolution can never be just about the seizure of political power and the control of state apparatus. The socialist revolution, and the revolution which Third Cinema aligns itself to, calls for an extension of the political revolution into a *social* revolution (Mèszàros, 1995). This means that every aspect of life must be transformed and democratised. Every microcosm of society – every organisation, institution, structure – must begin the hard work of organising its internal dynamics and practices and external relations with others on an entirely different basis than hitherto in the history of human kind: on the basis that is of control being vested with the majority. It is this kind of vision which Third Cinema aligns itself with because it is not just about making films, it has also experimented with altering the conditions of production and consumption; that is, within the social microcosm that is cinema, breaking down the hierarchical divisions of labour which cinema inherited from the capitalist society it, like the rest of us, grew up in. However, in Russia, by the late 1920s, it was clear that there was going to be no *social* revolution: the revolution had stopped (not least because of the failure of revolutions elsewhere to take hold) at the conquest of political power. And such a stunted revolution merely produces new exploiting elites.

MODERNISM, EISENSTEIN AND VERTOV

But in those early days, let us say the first decade after 1917, the revolution unleashed enormous cultural energies. Post-revolutionary Russia was the scene for an extraordinary cross-fertilisation between Marxism and modernism (although there were tensions and differences as well between the political avant-garde and the artistic avant-garde). Modernism impacted across the arts, including film, theatre, music, literature, typography and architecture. Composed of multiple strands (Cubism, Expressionism, Futurism, Dadaism, Surrealism, Constructivism) modernism is an umbrella term for a heterogeneous array of cultural practices, whose most important European geographical locations were Germany, Italy and Russia – both before and after the revolution.

Nevertheless, we can identify four characteristics which are frequently, if not always, at work within modernism. They are the technique of montage, self-reflexivity, the break with the past, and a fascination with modernity – particularly the city, new technology and the masses.

The principle of montage, that is juxtaposing disparate material, is evident across different strands of modernism. In terms of technique, montage is the thread which connects the shifting perspectives and collages of paint and newspaper on the Cubist canvases of Braque and Picasso, the incorporation of disparate materials (glass, wire, metal and so on) in Futurist sculptures, the Surrealist attempt to adopt the language of the unconscious, with its bizarre juxtapositions, and the editing of Eisenstein, with its emphasis on collision and shock for maximum emotional and intellectual stimulation. Leftist cultural practitioners saw a link between montage and social change. The emphasis which montage placed on the *construction* of meaning and perspective, on the arrangement of materials of the medium, suggested an analogy with the external world: that it too was a construct, that it too was assembled and could, through social revolution, be re-assembled along new lines.

However, montage not only suggested an analogy with the external world, it also threw the spectator's attention back to the artistic medium itself and to its own processes of assembling. Thus there is a close link between montage and a text's ability to comment on or draw attention to aspects of its own mode of production. The opening of Dziga Vertov's film *Man with a Movie Camera* (1929) begins inside a cinema where a film is about to be screened: the film is none other than *Man with a Movie Camera*. Later, the film cuts between an editor splicing the still images from the film together and the results of that labour as we 'return' to *Man with a Movie Camera*.

The self-reflexivity of modernism radically departed from the mimetic traditions of nineteenth-century art, which aspired to be a copy or passive reflection of the world. Applying modernist precepts to cinema, Vertov declared that: 'Up to today we *have coerced the film-camera and made it copy the work of our own eyes*. And the better the copying, the more highly was the shot considered. From today we are liberating the camera and making it work in the opposite direction, furthest away from copying' (1971/2:53).

Instead of being a copy, the text was now seen to be the product of human labour. Self-reflexivity turned the spectator's attention to the 'materiality' of the text, the fact that it is a product composed of codes and conventions and is the result of a labour process conducted under specific conditions. So here was another modernist bridge to Marxism. Firstly, self-reflexivity parallels the kind of investigation of foundational assumptions and procedures which is common in the social and political sciences generally. Secondly, discovering the cultural text to be a material product, the result of a labour process, chimed in to a certain extent with Marxism's socio-economic materialism.

There has however always been a danger and a tendency within European modernism for the text to become so obsessed with its own materiality, its own status as film or painting, that it forgets about the social world beyond its own signifiers. Yet, as Julianne Burton argues when assessing the importance of self-reflexivity for Third Cinema, this danger,

neither cancels out the importance of some filmmakers' commitment to saying *something* about the means of production of the film text *within* the film text, nor does it obviate the potential validity – even necessity – of a line of critical enquiry which takes material and social conditions of film's elaboration as its point of departure. (Burton, 1997:158)

One self-reflexive strategy that Third Cinema has often made use of is the film-within-a film structure. A film by the veteran Third Cinema filmmaker Jorge Sanjinés, called *The Bird's Singing* (1995), focuses on a film crew working in the high Bolivian plateau. They want to make a film about the arrival of the Spanish conquistadors in the sixteenth century but in their dealings with the Andean Indians they merely reproduce the colonialist domination which they want to make a critical film about. The Cuban film *The Elephant and the Bicycle* (Juan Carlos Tabio, 1995) explores the revolutionary possibilities of cinema by setting its story on an isolated island, seething with social discontent, to which a travelling cinema show has just arrived. Alternatively, Tabio's earlier film *Plaff* (1988) re-works Vertov's idea of opening with the projection of his own film. An intertitle tells us that *Plaff* was made in record time so that it would be completed for Filmmaker's Day. Yet when the film begins, the image is upside-down and soon disappears altogether. This is a sly dig at a command economy's production targets outweighing quality of production. A voice-over (the projectionist) declares that the reel is damaged and that he will have to send it back to ICAIC, the Cuban Film Institute, to be fixed. In the meantime, the film will have to start with the second reel.

The break with mimesis that self-reflexivity signals is part of a broader modernist rejection of the cultural past, its values as much as its techniques. The modernist emphasis on constructing the new obviously feeds into Birri's demand for a cinema which creates new people, new societies, new histories and new art (1997a:86–7). Nineteenth-century cultural values held up nature as a model of perfection which art should aspire to; there was the ideal of 'organic man' harmoniously relating to his social and natural environment and the unified, autonomous individual dominated literature and painting of the time. Such cultural values were felt by many modernists in the inter-war period to have been liquidated in the bloodshed of the First World War. In post-1917 Russia, a number of modernist artists, Futurists and Constructivists argued that their cultural practices represented a new true proletarian culture and that the entire bourgeois culture of the past could be consigned to the dustbin of history. However, despite the importance of revolution, of a fundamental break with what Marx called the 'traditions of all the dead generations' (1984:10), Marxism's attitude to the past is a good deal more complex and nuanced than the modernists'. The Bolshevik leader Leon Trotsky pointed out to those declaring the new arts to be the proper basis of a proletarian culture that since the masses had not yet had the leisure time or education to absorb the classic literature of bourgeois culture it was a mite premature to declare it as useless to the needs of the present. For Marxism, the past is not only a dead weight preventing the emergence of a future different from the present, the past is also the material and cultural prerequisite for that different future. (This is dialectical thinking.) There can be no socialism unless the productive forces are sufficiently developed so as to be able, once they are freed from the fetters of capital, to provide for all. And there can be no socialism unless the cultural level of the majority is sufficiently high to be able to deal with all the complexities of behaviour, attitude and intelligence that the *social* revolution would require.

Despite the modernist continuities, Third Cinema has a similarly more complex view of the past than the more dogmatic strands of European modernism. Perhaps this is because the specific history of colonialism and imperialism which wiped out or marginalised indigenous cultures in Latin America and Africa means that Third Cinema often displays a sense that these cultures have to be recovered/excavated, although also transformed, for the needs of the present. Another reason why the past cannot be ignored is that quite simply the struggles, the toil, the injustices and hopes of the majority of all the accumulated dead generations have yet to be redeemed (Benjamin, 1999:252). The discourse of 'modernisation' preached by capital's apparatchiks, from General Pinochet in Chile to Tony Blair in the UK, is precisely about trying to make people forget that such a redemption is owed; it is about trying to consign socialism to the dustbin of history and integrate us into a future from which there is no alternative. It is significant then that *Land and Freedom* (Ken Loach, 1995) begins in contemporary Britain before shifting back to the 1936 Spanish revolution. The film concludes back in contemporary Britain with the funeral of the central character. The presence of his granddaughter, who has found his letters and photos from Spain, the debris of history, makes explicit that there is a debt still to be paid to the struggles of the past.

The claim of some Russian modernists to be developing a culture of the masses arose naturally from their fascination with modernity whose characteristic icons were to be found in the city (as opposed to the natural landscapes of the Romantics), the masses (as opposed to the bourgeois individual) and new industrial technology (as opposed to the more primitive, artisanal labour celebrated by such nineteenth-century figures as John Ruskin, Thomas Carlyle and William Morris). Pre-war Italian Futurism had explicitly celebrated the machine age and its influence was to be turned in a more leftist, socially conscious direction by Russian Constructivism after the 1917 revolution. As Lunn notes, 'the machine became the model, or metaphor, for artistic creation itself' (1984:53). Thus in theatre Meyerhold developed a performance style called 'biomechanics' which adopted the movements and rhythms of the industrial age. Vertov celebrated the 'mechanical eye' of cinema:

> The mechanical eye: the film camera refusing to use the human eye as a crib, repelled and attracted by motions, gropes about in the chaos of visual events for the path for its own motion or oscillation, and experiments by stretching time, breaking up its motions, or, vice versa, absorbing time into itself, swallowing up the years, thereby schematizing prolonged processes which are inaccessible to the normal eye. (Vertov, 1971/2:56)

Constructivism's fascination with technology, industry and the masses could be articulated with the Marxist interest in the forces of production – the material basis for expanding the human capacity to shape and re-shape the natural and social world. However, less positively, the naïvely optimistic and somewhat uncritical attitude towards industry and production that Constructivism had inherited from Futurism was also converging with the decline of the revolution. Marxism also attaches great importance to *changing the social relations of production*. The how, why, where and when of production was supposed to be in the control of the producers themselves, not capital and its hierarchical command structure. However, the political context of Russia by the late 1920s was such that these ambitions were being snuffed out. This external political context, combined with Constructivism's unquestioning belief in the industrial age, is very evident in Vertov's *Man with a Movie Camera*. The film is a celebration of urban and industrial labour. In one (of many) virtuoso sequences, the film speeds up and intercuts between the assembly line of a cigarette factory and switchboard operators, before then cross-cutting on the motif of hands: hands working on a typewriter, hands on a piano, putting on make-up, a barber wiping the knife, an axe being sharpened, the camera handle being turned, and so on. Yet this celebration of the productive force of labour and its affinities to the machine fails to raise any questions about the *social relations* of labour: the divisions of labour and the hierarchical command structure under which labour functions remain unproblematised by the film. Made in the late 1920s, the film is a prisoner of its political context, when the social revolution was no longer on the agenda.

The modernism of Third Cinema has little time for the technological utopianism of these modernist strands (Willemen, 1989:12). It is less a modernism of clean lines and geometric shapes, of mechanical movements and depersonalised structures, rather if it has any links with European modernism, it is with the more sensuous tradition of surrealism; it is a modernism that lets the human body back into the equation and opens up a space for subjectivity, fantasy and the contradictions of desire.

An example of this more surreal modernism is found in *Touki Bouki*. Mori and his girlfriend Anta are planning to leave Senegal for France. Having visited a rich bourgeois former gay lover of Mori's, they steal clothes and money and trick the servant into giving them a lift in the elegant convertible (the car is a frequent symbol of western modernity in African cinema). The film then shades into a fantasy sequence. Mori, standing up in the car giving a speech, is intercut with footage of people lining the street for an actual procession. Thus the film makes use of the 'Kuleshov effect', whereby an association of spatial continuity or proximity is created by joining together footage from different scenes. A close-up of Mori and Anta, now all dressed up in sophisticated western suits, giving regal waves, is intercut with more footage of the procession, where official black Citroëns, horses and a band pass along the road. The fantasy continues, switching the scene to Mori and Anta's rural village where the people welcome them home and pay homage to them by singing and dancing. Mori and Anta, smoking and posing like white colonials, hand out money before driving off. The sequence dramatises Mori and Anta's dreams of a more materially comfortable life, but this is also mingled with a parody and critique of the African bourgeoisie and the mimicking of their former colonial masters.

The flourishing of revolutionary modernism in Russia was officially killed off in 1932 when the now Stalinised Communist Party imposed an official cultural line on the arts. This so-called

Socialist Realism was imposed in the name of making films that had the right ideological content, which Hollywood films did not, and were easily accessible to the masses, which the modernist experiments were not (Taylor, 1984). Essentially this involved the adoption of a classical narrative, individual heroes and positive and optimistic stories. The political conditions for a more complex engagement with the question of form, content and audiences no longer existed. The tension between militancy and entertainment, between engaging with popular culture and therefore mass audiences, while also seeking some transformation in consciousness and social reality, remains a central issue and problem for Third Cinema (Ngangura, 1996). This is a complex problem to which there is no single or easy answer. But the imposition of Socialist Realism from above by cultural bureaucrats is certainly a dead end. It is a problem that requires addressing the uneven cultural development between intellectuals and the masses, questions of finance, ownership and control of production, distribution and exhibition, and fluctuating political contexts in which possibilities for Third Cinema expand or contract.

LUKÁCS

Born in Hungary in 1885, Lukács's mother came from the nobility while his father occupied a senior position within the banking world. In the years before the First World War Lukács pursued a conventional academic career, steeping himself in the classical humanist culture of the nineteenth century, a culture he would never leave behind. Lukács felt profoundly alienated from the capitalist world around him, in particular (and this was a theme which was to dominate all his work) the world of capitalism was one in which the individual was isolated, unconnected and set in conflict with others and society in general.

Discontented, but as yet unable to identify any social force in the present that could bring about a better social order, Lukács nostalgically found inspiration in the great cultural heritage of Europe, stretching back to Greek epic literature. 'Against the inescapable human isolation and fragmented experience of the present, the early Lukács held up counter-images of classical organic harmony, the "whole man" fully alive in a unified community and natural world' (Lunn, 1984:92).

The outbreak of the First World War seemed to be the final confirmation of how far Europe had fallen from the cultural achievements of the past. Yet the Russian Revolution in 1917 gave Lukács renewed hope and propelled him into the study of Marxism. Here he found in the vision of the collective regaining control over their social environment, an image of unity, an image of reconciliation between individual and society, thought and reality, which had once seemed to be possible only as an aesthetic experience.

Although Lukács joined the Hungarian Communist Party after the 1917 revolution and later emigrated to the Soviet Union, he was, as my brief sketch of him thus far indicates, no champion of the modernist culture which briefly flowered there. There were two main reasons (an external reason and an internal one) why Lukács remained an unrepentant critic of modernist art throughout his life. Externally, the establishment of Socialist Realism in the Soviet Union and the rise of the Nazis in Germany abruptly stopped modernist culture in two of its main geographical centres in Europe. This meant that, particularly in the Soviet Union, there were no examples of modernist culture and no theoreticians to challenge Lukács at home. However, even if the political climate had been more favourable for modernism in the 1930s, Lukács would still not have championed modernism, for his aesthetic models were, as I have suggested, to be found in the past.

Lukács's relevance to us here does not then lie in his critique of modernism (which, as we shall see, is problematic) but in his critique of naturalism and aspects of his theory of realism in art. Clearly, as we saw in my analysis of *The Battle Of Algiers*, the question of realism is central to Third Cinema. Lukács found his inspiration for realism in the first flowering of the realist novel, prior to its demise into naturalism. The dates between which the novel was at the height of its realist power are significant: 1789–1848. The first date of course marks the outbreak of the French Revolution which swept away the political and moral corruption of aristocratic and monarchical rule. The nascent bourgeoisie was the key social force driving this revolution. In *The Communist Manifesto* Marx had paid tribute to the bourgeoisie for its initially progressive historic triumphs in sweeping away the remains of feudalism and developing science and technology. But in 1848, faced with European-wide uprisings of a now nascent working class, the period of the bourgeoisie as a progressive force came to an end in the suppression of the workers and the castigation of their demands. Instead, the bourgeoisie and the remnants of the aristocracy gave out 'the watch-words of the old society, *"property, family, religion, order"*, to the army as passwords and proclaimed... "By this sign thou shalt conquer!"' (Marx, 1984:19).

Literary realism became objectively (that is independent of the will of the author) less possible or likely or, at the least, badly compromised. The dominant political and social institutions mobilised to assert that capital was the finished and final form of society. There could be no alternatives. This situation seeps into the very pores of literary representation, transforming realism into naturalism. While the realist novel (for example, Scott, Tolstoy, Balzac) during the period of revolutionary bourgeois change developed aesthetic strategies particularly attuned to grasping society as a *process*, naturalism, at best, can only manage a horrified but resigned depiction of a society already finished, complete and unalterable. This however is only a surface appearance. History never stops and a key feature of the social world is that it is always in 'infinite process' (Lukács, 1978:27). Any representation that tries to fix or eternalise the social world, or is fixated on 'accidental, ephemeral, contingent phenomena' is an inadequate 'photographic reproduction of the immediately perceptible superfice of the external world' (1978:75).

Certainly, one element of my critique of *The Battle of Algiers* was that it had overly invested in getting the immediate appearance of the real in the raw with its imitation of 1960s reportage, and that not enough attention had been paid to deeper, more fundamental dynamics. Lukács's idea that the social world is in process and that realist art must 'uncover the deeper, hidden, mediated, not immediately perceptible network of relationships that go to make up society' (1988:38), anticipates Espinosa's call for Third Cinema to 'show the process which generates the problems' (1997:81).

Lukács's emphasis on (slowly) discovering the network of relationships derives from the classic realist novel, with its careful delineation of a wide range of characters, the elaboration of their interrelationships and the gradual manner in which the novel ratchets up the intensity and significance of their interactions. It was this attachment to the classic realist novel as the *only* form suitable for realism which limited Lukács's cultural criticism and would have made him hostile to the work of all modernism, including Eisenstein.

In *October* (1927) Eisenstein rapidly draws the connections between the different components of the ruling classes in the scene of the massacre around the bridges of St Petersburg. Using montage, Eisenstein juxtaposes the bourgeois press, the army and middle-class pleasure seekers along the river. The spectator is asked to instantly draw the connection between the 'ruling ideas' propagated by the press, armed force and social privilege. It is a masterful sequence and certainly one which articulates the 'deeper, hidden...not immediately perceptible network of relationships'. Lukács though would have felt it was too crude, too abrupt, not sufficiently mediated – which is to say he would have wanted a more gradual elaboration of the interactions between the social forces depicted. It is through that interaction that the realist work delineates character – for individuation was a key category for Lukács.

Closely linked with naturalism's inability to give adequate representation to the deep underlying social forces at work is naturalism's penchant for description and obsession with detail. The immaculate recording of the surface details of life can be read as a displacement, an overcompensation for being unable to represent any of the processes that generate the problems. Description is also linked to the naturalistic tendency to aspire towards a kind of narrational neutrality. At the level of aesthetics, this often manifests itself with attempts to make the act of narration, the act of story-telling, appear as invisible or as transparent as possible. As the act of storytelling becomes invisible, so the *standpoint* from which the events are told also acquires a pseudo-impartiality.

Lukács posited the realist novel against these characteristics of naturalism (the lack of underlying causes, description for the sake of description and a neutral or impartial standpoint on the story-action). Now the novel as a model has a number of characteristics and some aspects of Lukács's theory of realism seem inextricably tied to those characteristics. But there are concepts in Lukács's theory which can be prised away from being exclusively true of his preferred aesthetic model and applied more generally to many other forms of realism. Two concepts in particular seem especially pertinent: they are typicality and totality.

Lukács on typicality: 'What characterizes the type is the convergence and intersection of all...the most important social, moral and spiritual contradictions of a time...Through the creation of the type and the discovery of typical characters and typical situations, the most significant directions of social development obtain adequate artistic expression' (1978:78).

So, in the typical situation and typical character, realism articulates the key, significant dynamic forces that are at work in society.
Through the typical, realism finds the nodal points through which
'the major opposing forces converge' (Lukács, 1978:142). Typicality
should not be confused with the vernacular 'that's typical'. For
Lukács, it means something quite different from the ordinary, the
everyday, the average. Indeed it is naturalism that is characterised
by the obsession with the quotidian. In the representation of the
average, important social contradictions 'lose their decisiveness'
(1978:78).

The distinction between the average and the typical can be
brought out by a number of cinematic examples. Take for example
the plight of Ricci in Vittorio de Sica's classic Italian neorealist film
Bicycle Thieves (1948). In my discussion of *The Battle of Algiers* I noted
how important neorealism was for that film and indeed for many
Second Cinema films that attempt to engage with the brutal realities
of life. Neorealism was also influential on Third Cinema filmmakers,
but it was an aesthetic that had to be profoundly reworked because
of its naturalistic limitations (Hess, 1993). Those limitations are
evident in *Bicycle Thieves*. Ricci is one of the many unemployed in
postwar Italy. Thus potentially he could be a typical character since
unemployment is certainly a site where the social contradictions of
the time converge. However, to become a typical character, Ricci's
story would have to be interwoven into the more general social
forces at work. Yet he remains resolutely cut off from the wider
collective – even at the beginning, when we first see him, he is not
with the men clamouring outside the unemployment exchange.
Instead he is separated from them, sitting on the pavement across
the street and has to be called over by someone who knows him
when his name is called out. He is offered the job of a flyposter,
which depends on his reclaiming his bicycle from the pawn shop.
This he does, but the bicycle is stolen from him on his first day
(while he is putting up a poster of Rita Hayworth, a Second Cinema
dig at First Cinema's remoteness from the actual lives of ordinary
people). The rest of the film is composed of a wandering and
ultimately fruitless search through Rome with his son, Bruno.
Nothing *decisive* happens because Ricci is cut off from the broader
social forces that surround him.

Ousmane Sembene's film *Xala* (1974) demonstrates typicality of
situations and characters. The film concerns a business man and
political leader (El Hadji) in a newly independent African country

(Sembene's own Senegal). The Xala is the curse of impotence which has struck El Hadji on the night of his wedding to his third wife. This impotence is not just sexual or individual (the province of First and Second Cinema), it stands in for the political and economic impotence of his class. This is demonstrated in the brilliantly economic and satirical opening sequence.

The film begins with celebrations of national liberation taking place out in the streets. The liberation leaders (including El Hadji) mount the stairs to the Chamber of Commerce, cheered on by the crowd. (Interestingly, the editing here suggests proximity between the leaders and the crowd in the manner of Kuleshov's creative geography. We do not actually see the crowd and the leaders together in the same shot – perhaps this is an indication that the links between the crowd and the leaders are more tenuous than a long shot/establishing shot would suggest.) A diegetic but asyn-chronic voice-over from the new President tells how important it is that African countries control their industry, commerce and culture. The liberation leaders enter the offices of the Chamber where three white businessmen are sitting. The leaders unceremoniously remove icons of French domination from the office (military boots and hats, busts – the *mise-en-scène* is non-naturalistic) and place them on the steps of the Chambers. The crowd continue their chanting, playing the drums and so on. The leaders return to the office and wordlessly gesture to the French colonials to leave. This they do without protest (perhaps reassured by the voice-over at this moment which is declaring the new leaders to be businessmen, and that the struggle for liberation is over). The colonials leave the building, taking their icons with them; the leaders soak up more of the crowd's joy before returning inside. A brief ellipsis and we find the French officials returning. The first is accompanied by black soldiers who begin, on his command, to push the crowd back. The other two French officials now appear, each clutching several briefcases. Inside the bank, the leaders are now dressed in business suits and formal dinner dress (they are going to El Hadji's wedding). They are sitting around the table when the French return. A briefcase is placed in front of each one. They peek inside, nod in approval and, with what Brecht would have called a gestus (a socially significant gesture), place their arms protectively over the case. Then the President opens his case: it is stuffed with money. Does he protest? No. Instead he stands up and gives a speech about the virtues of their revolution. Everyone applauds, including the French bankers.

These are typical characters in typical situations – as Lukács understood the term. Again and again, the historical record shows how black liberation leaders, ignoring Fanon's warnings, came to power, captured the state and parts of the economy, and turned themselves into the new élites, the new personifications of capital. The revolution is limited merely to the political sphere. As an example of Third Cinema, *Xala* does not become the mouthpiece and propagandist of the new élites, but instead asks what has happened to those who remain socially disenfranchised because the revolution has not involved a broader social transformation.

The other concept that I think is broadly relevant to different forms of realism, far beyond Lukács's early nineteenth-century literary model, is that of totality. This concept means 'microcosm'. A microcosm is something that has all the essential features of a larger entity but boiled or compressed down into a smaller unit. The larger entity in this case is the 'extensive totality of life' (Lukács, 1978:38). However, to try to grasp and represent the entire world external to the text is neither possible nor desirable. Instead, the text must structure and order, select and compress the extensive totality of life itself into the intensive totality which is the literary or, in our case, cinematic text. One simple question which we can ask of a text in order to gauge whether it has achieved a representation of the social totality is whether it brings into representation the conflicting social classes and their organisations.

On the face of it, *Bicycle Thieves* does represent something of the social totality. In his journey through Rome, Ricci comes into contact with the unemployed, the unemployment exchange, the pawnshop, the police, the church, the trade union, a mystic, thieves, workers and so on. This sounds like a fairly broad canvas of social forces and groups. But the concept of the totality also implies something else: that the realist text seek out the interconnections and relations (including the conflictual relations) *within* the social totality and between these social groups, in order to show life as a process. Naturalism however turns a 'representation of life in motion into a description of more or less static conditions' (Lukács, 1978:164). And this is precisely the limitation of *Bicycle Thieves*. Ricci comes into momentary contact with all these groups, but there is no attempt to weave the social connections between them. The film is unable to show them as anything but components of a world that are isolated from one another. The film cannot make connections, cannot delve beneath the surface of life which remains, as it always does within the naturalist aesthetic, chaotic, full of contingent, ephemeral and transient actions.

It cannot be stressed enough that the notion of figuring the social totality is not a quantitative one. In terms of film time, the standardised length of 90 minutes is no restriction on realist aspirations. Figuring the totality is a question of composition, of structuring and arranging the material. With the right compositional strategies and antennae for the socially significant, one can do an awful lot in ten minutes of screen time. With the wrong strategies and with no eye for what is socially resonant, a film can do very little, even if it ran for 100 hours. A ten-minute sequence from *Xala* illustrates this.

It is the day after El Hadji's wedding. His import and export shop is being opened by his secretary. She notes a 'bad smell' in the place. Cut to an exterior shot of women pouring their dirty water down a drain hole. Inside, the secretary, spraying perfumed water, observes and is disgusted, blaming the women for the smell. It is not the poverty she objects to but the women themselves. The spectator, however, suspects that the smell has more to do with corruption (El Hadji has diverted public money to pay for his wedding). Meanwhile a young man sells the secretary a journal called *Kaddu*, the only journal in the indigenous language (Wolof). As she starts work, some beggars arrive and begin playing their music outside. Then El Hadji arrives by car. He tells the secretary to call the President. Cut to exterior shot and more beggars and cripples are shown moving along the streets. On the soundtrack we overhear a car accident. Cut to the crowd scene surrounding the accident. On the periphery of the crowd a man is having his wallet stolen by a thief. We cut back to the President's car arriving at El Hadji's office. El Hadji tells him of the Xala. But when asked who cursed him, El Hadji does not respond. Instead he gets up and goes to the window where he can hear the music of the beggars and cripples. He demands the President get rid of this 'human rubbish'. The President makes a phone call and then advises El Hadji to see a witch doctor. The film then cuts to the man who was robbed. He is explaining to the young man selling *Kaddu* that the money stolen belonged to his village, which was already suffering from crop failures. As he tells his story, the film cuts to shots of police vans arriving with the soldiers. They arrest both of them and brusquely round up the beggars. The sequence ends with the thief who stole the money entering a tailor's. An ellipsis and the man reappears wearing a smart business suit and an American, perhaps Texan-style hat.

Using a geographical location (El Hadji's shop and its immediate surrounds) the film draws the interactions between a cross-section of the social body. The political and business élites respond to the masses they have betrayed with fear and hatred, displacing their own corruption onto them (the 'bad smell' the 'human rubbish'). Greedily appropriating the icons of wealth and modernity (the cars), the élites also cling onto the most reactionary elements of African culture (polygamy and witch doctors). An interest in a culture that synthesises the best of native and international culture (*Kaddu* takes the form of a journal, but in Wolof) is as much a threat as the poor (hence the *Kaddu* seller's arrest). The street thief is a smaller version of El Hadji, stealing from the masses and then aping the attire of the rich and exploiting west.

BRECHT AND BENJAMIN

To see modernist culture as merely the culture of the intelligentsia – the charge with which Soviet Socialist Realism quashed modernist cultural production – is profoundly undialectical. Lukács's critique of modernism was a good deal more sophisticated – although he did also charge modernism as being out of touch with the popular culture of the masses – but ultimately it served to buttress his own aesthetic preferences and failed to grasp the significance of modernism. The reason why modernism could not and cannot be dismissed as simply the cultural capital of the intelligentsia is that it articulates aspects of the lived experience of the urban masses in industrial capitalism and mass culture. Benjamin and Brecht understood this, perhaps more than anyone. They detected within the industrial and cultural forms of modernity new potentialities: collective identities, the capacity to make connections swiftly between spatially different phenomena, a critical, sceptical attitude, a thirst for information, a willingness to innovate, and so on. They also recognised that the socioeconomic and cultural forces of modernity could brutalise, mystify and manipulate the masses. The technologies of cultural production – particularly the recent technologies of photography, film and radio – were key sites where these potentialities could be pulled and developed one way or another, positive or negative, socialist or capitalist/fascist. Lukács's almost exclusive focus on traditional literature offered little help in this struggle. But modernism offered a set of cultural resources and strategies that could potentially develop a socialist consciousness embryonic within modern life.

Although Brecht was prepared to utilise modernist strategies, he was also prepared to engage with popular forms. His definition of realism is interesting for its refusal to stipulate any *formal* strategies as intrinsically realist or unrealistic.

> Realistic means: discovering the causal complexes of society/unmasking the prevailing view of things as the view of those who are in power/writing from the standpoint of the class which offers the broadest solutions for the pressing difficulties in which human society is caught up/emphasizing the element of development/making possible the concrete, and making possible abstraction from it. (Brecht, 1988:82)

This is a political definition of realism which makes no assumptions concerning which aesthetic strategies can or cannot be used. Brecht was here criticising Lukács's iron attachment to the aesthetic strategies of the bourgeois novel, advocating instead a much more flexible response to the *potential* of all cultural forms. Again this anticipates the hybrid character of much of Third Cinema, with its engagement with popular and modernist cultural forms.

During the 1930s the Marxist philosopher Walter Benjamin advocated and developed many of Brecht's ideas concerning cultural production. In his essay on Brecht's Epic Theatre, Benjamin noted how clear and communicative it is (1999a:144), even using the word 'pellucid' which prefigures Espinosa's call for a lucid cinema for lucid people, 'who think and feel and exist in a world which they can change' (Espinosa, 1997:80). Such lucidity though requires reworking the ratio between emotional and intellectual stimulation which is the norm for dominant theatre and film. As Willemen notes, 'the culture industry has become extremely adept at orchestrating emotionality while deliberately atrophying the desire for understanding and intellectuality' (Willemen, 1989:13). This does not mean that Third Cinema aspires to be an emotional vacuum, far from it. Without the emotions of anger, outrage, passion, there can be little desire to change the world. But certainly, Third Cinema seeks to achieve a new synthesis between the spectator's emotional and intellectual capacities. Brecht's drama prefigures this ambition because, as Benjamin notes, it 'eliminated the Aristotelian catharsis, the purging of the emotions through empathy with the stirring fate of the hero' (Benjamin, 1999a:147). Typically, Brecht's Epic Theatre produces 'astonishment rather than empathy' (1999a:147), so that the spectator asks: is this how things really are? how can things be so absurd or unjust? Epic theatre places an emphasis on the discovery of the conditions of life.

In 'The Author as Producer' Benjamin develops Brechtian ideas across cultural production generally. For Benjamin a 'producer' is a cultural worker who produces material that resists assimilation to the apparatus of production. By contrast, a cultural hack is someone 'who refuses as a matter of principle to improve the production apparatus and so prise it away from the ruling class' (Benjamin, 1982:23). He begins by arguing that political commitment is a question, above all, of 'technique'. In foregrounding the importance of technique, that is the techniques or conventions of composition, Benjamin is emphasising the specificity of the cultural artifact – a theme, as we have already seen, of modernist culture. Thus in my analysis of *The Battle of Algiers* I suggested that Gillo Pontecorvo's own personal commitment to the anti-colonial struggle is one thing; but the techniques or aesthetic strategies which the film mobilises undermine the analytical, cognitive potential of the commitment of all those involved.

Benjamin continues his argument concerning techniques by advocating that cultural producers break down the divisions between the techniques clustered around and between mediums. '[W]e must rethink the notions of literary forms or genres if we are to find forms appropriate to the literary energy of our time' (1982:18).

Thus he praises Brecht's theatre for drawing on new mass media forms (radio, film, photography and the press). This emphasis on new combinations and breaking down divisions between mediums and genres is part of a larger argument about subverting the production apparatus. This should also involve not just questions of cultural form, but also the breaking down of the divisions of labour within the production process – where techniques are parcelled to different roles (director, producer, writer, camera operator and so on) as well as the divisions between those who produce culture and those who consume it. A number of themes here prefigure Third Cinema concerns – democratising production, encouraging a more 'active' spectator and the attention paid to reworking the meaning or politics of techniques, giving them a 'functional transformation' (1982:22). Brecht's and Benjamin's concern is to prick the political conscience of the intelligentsia, arguing that they 'should not supply the production apparatus without, at the same time, within the limits of the possible, changing that apparatus in the direction of socialism' (1982:22).

Of course, there may be a lot of disagreement on what constitues the 'limits of the possible' at any one time. Pontecorvo for example might have argued that *The Battle of Algiers* represented the limits of the possible at the time of its production. I think however that such a defence still fails to engage with the politics of technique and the necessity for the functional transformation of techniques. The real proof however that *The Battle of Algiers* does not represent the limits of the possible and that political commitment is above all articulated at the level of technique is Pontecorvo's own film *Burn* (1968), which he made after *The Battle of Algiers*. *Burn* is a marked change of aesthetic direction for Pontecorvo. Made in colour, it appropriates the epic swashbuckler genre and grafts it onto a mid-nineteenth century tale of the struggle between English and Portuguese colonialism to control sugar in the Caribbean and the struggle of the natives against their masters. The dialogue and the action foregrounds precisely what is missing from *The Battle of Algiers*: economics, profits, the bourgeoisie, political manoeuvring by western powers and the growth in political consciousness of the exploited. Unlike *The Battle of Algiers*, this film does not deploy representational techniques which imitate documentary. Thus *Burn* is able to invest its situations and characters with great typicality, in the Lukácsian sense. Pontecorvo's masterstroke is to employ an illiterate Colombian cane-cutter in the part of the rebel leader, José, and cast him opposite the greatest actor of his generation, Marlon Brando.

Brando plays the English spy Sir William Walker who arrives on the island of Queimada to foment a native revolution against the Portuguese rulers. Once this is achieved the English put in place a bourgeois mulatto as their puppet ruler. Walker leaves the island, only to return ten years later to put down a new rebellion, led by José, against English capital. To defeat José, most of the island is burnt by Walker (an allusion to the American policy of using napalm in Vietnam). *Burn* brilliantly subverts the technique of identification. As Danny Peary notes, Brando/Walker is for the first half of the film 'our hero. Pragmatic, intellectual, witty. He seems to genuinely like José and to be concerned about the plight of the blacks on Queimada' (1982:43). Gradually, however, the spectator realises that Walker cannot rise above his historical and class location within the colonial apparatus, and that his cynical amoralism conceals his own paralysis: he knows that the economic interests he fights for are vile, but he cannot commit himself to the black struggle. Thus the film is one of those rare achievements: a critique of the star system using a star, the mechanisms of identification, the hierarchy between actors, the spectator's need for a powerful ego-ideal to empathise with in a relatively uncomplicated way, the star as narrative agent to resolve problems – all these techniques, the film unravels.

Pontecorvo then achieves in *Burn* what he fails to achieve in *The Battle of Algiers*: the 'functional transformation' of the cultural production apparatus which Brecht and Benjamin were arguing for. In 'The Author as Producer' Benjamin offers a critique of the German cultural movement called 'New Objectivity'. A reaction to the subjectivism and fantastic qualities of German Expressionism, New Objectivity specialised in representing the working class in a naturalistic manner. Thus it distinguishes itself from the 'mass media' in the same way that Second Cinema distinguishes itself from First Cinema – by addressing those areas of life marginalised or ignored by the dominant media. Benjamin however critiqued New Objectivity's influence on photography, arguing that it turned reportage into a modish fashion, while 'turning abject poverty itself, by handling it in a modish, technically perfect way, into an object of enjoyment' (1982:24). Here Benjamin identifies a contradiction between intention and effect and between content (poverty, hardship) and form or technique. Benjamin praises Brecht's strategy of stripping away all the paraphernalia of theatrical spectacle. 'He confined himself, as it were, to a podium, a platform. He renounced plots requiring a great deal of space' (1982:28). This prefigures Espinosa's refusal to let the technical standards of dominant cinema dictate what a film should look like. Many Third Cinema films (although certainly not all) are, relatively speaking, financially poor but this contributes to their being culturally rich. It is not that Third Cinema fetishises poverty of cultural production, rather it is a question of what is appropriate to the work being undertaken. The cultural producer must be aware of the economic relations underpinning an apparatus built around spectacle, and ask whether that is to be rejected or, as in *Burn*, deconstructed.

The most intense area for innovation and experimentation within First Cinema today is in the field and industry of special effects – that is, precisely, in intensifying the spectacle of First Cinema. Rejecting this one-sided development of the medium, Third Cinema has a very different sense of the experimental, prefigured once more in Benjamin's call for cultural production to take on the character of a 'dramatic laboratory rather than a finished work of art' (1982:29). Benjamin's essay, above all else, asks the cultural producer, 'to *think*, to reflect upon his position in the production process' (1982:29).

We have seen then in this chapter that many of the theories and practices that define Third Cinema were formulated in the work of key Marxists across a range of mediums in the 1920s and 1930s. We have seen that Third Cinema, in some instances, marks an advance on the work of those thinkers; for example, Lukács's attachment to past cultural forms and the modernist suspicion of past cultural forms. Perhaps most importantly, Third Cinema is the beneficiary, 40, 50 and more years on, of a higher cultural level of the masses, and a greater sophistication and familiarity with cinema. It is still of course a cinema dominated by First Cinema but that cinema cannot ignore the accumulating social problems that the economic order in which it is embedded generates. And it is a cinema dimly aware of its internal problems and limitations and of the existence of alternatives. This is why we find examples of progressive films within First Cinema. It is the dialectical struggle (interaction, appropriation, negation) between such films and Third Cinema to which we now must turn.

3 Dialectics of First and Third Cinema

This chapter explores the critique of First Cinema by Third Cinema in more detail. I have argued that films often draw on the influences of First, Second and Third Cinema. Yet they nevertheless transform the influences of the other two cinemas into the terms and principles of one cinema, whether it is First, Second or Third. This indeed is part of the dialectics which I wish to explore. The critique of First Cinema by Third Cinema covers both infrastructural questions of production, distribution and exhibition as well as aesthetic issues concerning the films themselves. We will begin with the question of production, how it is organised and for what purposes, and explore the relationship between the process of production and the film text. Then I explore in more detail a critique of the politics of First Cinema's aesthetic strategies using some of the critical terms with which I discussed *The Battle of Algiers* (historicity, politicisation, commitment and cultural specificity). Finally, I will address the infrastructural questions of distribution and exhibition.

RELATIONS OF PRODUCTION

Third Cinema has pioneered democratic modes of production that have sought to break down the divisions of labour and hierarchies of command which the film industry, as a microcosm of the social totality, has institutionalised. However, we do need to be clear about the limits of the immediate context of production on determining the question: is this film or television text an example of Third Cinema? It is possible for a production process to develop a more collective, non-hierarchical mode but this does not *in itself* guarantee that the film which emerges from this process will be a Third Cinema text. It may make it more likely – but that is all. The key issue, recalling the arguments advanced so far, is whether the techniques, as Benjamin calls them, of representation have been worked on in a way that is adequate to a revolutionary politics. These techniques, as a set of cultural resources, already preexist the moment of production. If in the process of production a particular set of techniques are mobilised without an adequate understanding of their 'politics', then it may well be that a more democratic and collective mode of production will not produce a Third Cinema text. Conversely, it is possible – although it has to be said, it is rare – for a film to be made in the jaws of the most ferociously capital-dominated culture industry in the world and still be regarded as an example of Third Cinema. I will argue in the final chapter that this is indeed the case for *Evita* (1996), despite the fact that it was a Hollywood production made by people not known for their revolutionary views. Nevertheless, although the production process does not offer any guarantees, developing alternative modes of production remains an essential contribution to a broader democratic project.

COLLECTIVE PRODUCTION IN THE UK

Within the UK the longest-running and most successful attempt to develop an alternative mode of cultural production can be found in Newcastle. Amber Films was set up in the late 1960s as a non-profit-making collective. For more than three decades Amber have worked to put down deep roots in the regional culture of the north-east. While from a national perspective Amber have been largely ignored, they represent possibly the most successful 'studio' – in terms of sheer longevity – in British film history. The work of Amber is very diverse, but what it shares, across a range of output, is a concern to represent the culture and lives of the working class in the north-east region. Amber have over the years established a photographic gallery, a cinema and a working pub (also used as a film set). They work in film, television, theatre and photography. Their film work was initially exclusively documentary but gradually they have broadened the repertoire and have experimented with a fusion of documentary and fiction. Since the films are about the lives of local people, Amber work closely with them, involving them in the production process.

Whether this Third Cinema mode of production produces Third Cinema films is an interesting question and perhaps, given the diversity of output, impossible to give a general answer to. There is a strong naturalistic current to much of their work (for example, *Seacoal* (1985) and *In Fading Light* (1989)), but there are also modernist experiments such as *T. Dan Smith* (1987) with its self-reflexive documentary film-within-a-fictional-film structure, while *Dream On* (1991) uses surrealism to articulate working-class desires. Nevertheless, at the risk of an unfair generalisation, the determinedly regional focus of their work and the particularity with which they explore specific groups often militates against telling a story invested with the broader political and social significance that characterises Third Cinema. Although cultural specificity is an important component of Third Cinema, specificity and particularity must also be reconnected to the *general* processes of our times: a reconciliation which Lukács argued was essential to realism for the very reason that capitalism encourages modes of thinking and representation in which the *connections* between events and situations remain opaque. This is so, because right at the heart of the mode of production the *connection* between labour and the products which it produces has been severed and expropriated by capital. Thus our social relationships take on the *appearance* of 'things' (as Marx described them): inert, isolated, given, external to us and beyond our control. And one manifestation of this situation where 'a definite social relation between men assumes in their eyes the fantastic form of a relation between things' (Marx, 1967:77) is when particularities struggle to resonate and communicate to us their *broader* social significance.

A recent experiment by the television dramatist Jimmy McGovern also gives an indication of the dissatisfaction with conventional modes of working practices within the dominant audio-visual industry. McGovern, the writer of television dramas such as *Cracker*, *The Lakes* and *Hillsborough*, collaborated with the sacked Liverpool dockers to write *Dockers* (1999). This was a dramatisation of the 28 month campaign after 500 dockers were sacked by the Mersey Docks and Harbour Company in 1995 for refusing to cross a picket line mounted by workers from a rival firm after a dispute about casual labour. The collaboration was a learning experience for both parties. The writing group, made up of dockers and their wives, learned crucial skills of dramatic writing. McGovern meanwhile was able to hone a script which had been generated by those who had been at the heart of the dispute. This gave the drama a political coherence and toughness which, judging from McGovern's other work, he would not have been able to articulate as the sole author. The unique collective nature of the project is recognised in the credits, where McGovern (and Irvine Welsh, who also helped) are listed in alphabetical order along with 14 other scriptwriters.

Although it is impossible to prove one way or another whether *Dockers* would have been significantly different had it been produced through more conventional processes, it is reasonable to suggest that the self-dramatisation of the dockers by the dockers gives an authenticity to the drama which a more distanced approach – even if sympathetic – would have missed.

A good example of how the dockers' own perspective on the strike comes through in the drama concerns their understanding of its social significance. The dispute had received little attention from the media because it was seen as so old-fashioned: a strike involving manual workers in a declining industry, it seemed, in the discourse of New Labour, so *old labour*. This is directly addressed by one of the characters, the wife of a docker who has gone to speak to a group of teachers. Identifying how the experience of the dockers is a microcosm of the casualisation, insecurity and lack of rights sweeping through both working- and middle-class jobs, she notes that 'this is the most modern dispute imaginable.' Unlike *The Battle of Algiers*, the drama also explores how the involvement of women in social struggle transforms them and their relationship with their men. When she returns home elated by her success in speaking publicly for the first time, her husband is angry and resentful that he has been left at home, cast in the usual domestic role of the woman just at the time when the key source of his identity – his work – has been taken away from him. The impact of social struggle on gender relations and the role and contribution of women in the struggle against exploitation is a key theme for Third Cinema.

The other element to *Dockers* that is unusual in television and which might have been played down in another version of the story is the role of the dockers union the TGWU and, in particular, its general secretary, Bill Morris. *Dockers* is very clear about making a distinction between the union as the principal and practical embodiment of collective strength (which the dockers believe in) and the *union leadership* as a force which undermines and blocks the solidarity upon which unions have historically relied. Central to the tragedy of *Dockers* is that the strikers could have won reinstatement had the trade union leadership given them official backing. Fearing that a high-profile strike would turn the media against New Labour (then in opposition) or that the union might have funds seized by the courts through anti-trade union legislation, the union leadership preferred to sacrifice the dockers on the altar of 'realism' and moderation. In response to the drama, a spokesperson for Bill Morris argued that: 'The general secretary had to take account of the whole union. The actions the dockers took threatened its survival' (Gibbons, 1999:10). The best response to this argument comes from within the drama itself – which is a testimony to its political strength. Towards the end, the dockers' representative speaks at the TGWU conference, hoping to win delegates over, against the recommendation from the leadership, to supporting the strike.

> The General Secretary bangs on about the fabric of the union. That the union *might* get sued and that the fabric of the union might get damaged. What is the fabric of the union, eh? Is it this? (gestures to the building) Is it the General Secretary's posh office? Is it his posh car? Is it his chauffeur? No. The fabric of the union is the membership (applause). What is the fundamental principle of the union? The strength of the many will protect the few. Well, you are the many and we are the few – and you're *not* protecting us. Look at all this. A whole institution has been built around the principle of the many protecting the few, and you're proud of that institution, so proud, that 500 dockers can go and rot, just so long as you can hold on to the building, the offices and the mobile fucking phones. We were dismissed for refusing to cross a picket line. I am proud to say that we did not cross a picket line, because if people had crossed picket lines in the past, there would be no trade union movement.

Although the delegates are won round to voting for the motion to support the dockers, the leadership, in a stunning act of contempt, simply ignored the vote. The trenchant and reiterated critique of the trade union leadership and its disastrous consequences for the dockers is reminiscent of the work and rank-and-file politics of Ken Loach, particularly the television drama *Days of Hope*. The strength of *Dockers* over some of the work (fine though it is) produced by Amber is that it does manage to link the struggles of a particular group into the more general (*mise-en)scène* of national politics. Yet while *Dockers* is a fine testimony to the strengths of collaborative production, the television apparatus that commissioned it can only contemplate this sort of work on a very infrequent basis. The idea of collective, collaborative productions, giving grass roots voices access to a wide audience, is simply something which cannot be accommodated within the social relations of televisual production. For it raises too many questions about the hierarchical mode of production, about who television is responsible to, about what constitutes good television and about the acceptable range of views to gain air time.

BOORMAN AND *THE EMERALD FOREST*

The collective process that McGovern submitted himself to in the writing of *Dockers* compares favourably with the mode of production for the film *The Emerald Forest* (1985) directed by John Boorman. The film concerns an American engineer, Markham, working on a dam project in Brazil. When his young son is kidnapped by an Indian tribe he spends the next ten years searching for him. When Markham finds his son, Tommy, he has become a fully indigenised member of the Indian tribe and cannot return to Markham's world. The jungle and Tommy's world is threatened by the encroaching modernisation symbolised by the dam and so Markham must reassess his beliefs and loyalties to 'progress'. *The Emerald Forest* was one of the first mainstream films to tap into the growing concern with the politics of the environment – at least as a problem that existed in the here and now (the science fiction film *Soylent Green* (Richard Fleischer) anticipated environmental breakdown in 2022 – back in 1973). It is a useful text for us because Boorman published a diary on the making of the film which provides source material for an insight into the dominant mode of production.

The title of the diary is *Money into Light* and this is significant. For Boorman is not a contract director appointed to a project by studio heads. Rather, the story which became the film is one which Boorman has to feel personally committed to, a commitment which helps sustain him in the hard work of generating financial backing from the reluctant money men. Boorman has little affinity with Hollywood; Los Angeles is 'phoney as hell' a place that has 'betrayed the human spirit' (1985:1–2). Thus the diary is a story about the struggle to turn money and all the debilitating values it represents into not just film but *light*, something ethereal, transcendent and magical. Boorman, then, is a Second Cinema director working, in this instance, within First Cinema. One of the themes that links his work is an interest in the archaic, the mythical, the other-worldly. Throughout the book Boorman plays the auteur by linking *The Emerald Forest* to his body of work and its thematic continuities. 'We all have a landscape of the spirit, that place in which we feel – not peace but wholeness. Mine is the forest: but northern oak and beech woods. I filmed much of *Excalibur* in one of the few primeval oak forests left in Europe, uncut and unplanted' (1985:50).

This interest in the archaic and the mythic is a coded critique of capitalism – a word Boorman never uses. For to name in concrete, historical terms the social order from which he is so alienated would require him to come out from the shell of the individual artist and engage in a world where other people are struggling to change the very world he finds so appalling. Boorman's mobilisation of myth has the double advantage of both sounding properly 'artistic' and anti-commercial while also avoiding historical and cultural specificity. Boorman writes that myth transcends psychological and political realism, constructing instead archetypes embedded in the human psyche (1985:22–3). However, the notion of archetypes that transcend history is absolutely compatible with First Cinema which likes nothing better than to dissolve the historical specificity of social problems since that implies that they are not problems intrinsic to a mode of production dominated by capital.

While Boorman is clearly concerned and sincere his film practice is badly compromised by the mode of production of First Cinema. For while the diary concentrates on *his* struggle to turn money into light, this is not in fact the end of the circuit of capital. Marx (1983:145–53) identified the formula which expresses the circuit of capital as an endless cycle of money-into-commodity-into-money (M-C-M). Thus Boorman and the film are enmeshed in a set of social dynamics in which the circuit of capital requires the 'light' (or, in less mystical terms, the commodity) *to be turned back into money (profit)*. The anticipation that *The Emerald Forest* must, as a commodity, conform to this logic inscribes itself into the *techniques* (Benjamin) that the film uses and fails to submit to any analysis or critique. Money into light. Light into money.

Thus for example the film reproduces the typical western split in perceiving the other. We have the good noble Indians, the Invisible People, and we have the bad savage Indians, the so called Fierce People. As if this simple dualism – so second nature to the classical narrative structure – was not bad enough, the Fierce People just so happen to be black, while the good Indians are white – a good example of a liberal film unthinkingly reproducing racist stereotypes. The story of the relationship between father and son is a variant on the Oedipal drama which has been the mainstay of Hollywood films from the 1950s at least. It is their relationship that fills out the narrative space of the film, making it impossible to represent them within a larger social totality. Dam construction is one of the most common means by which political and economic élites in the third world connect financially with the political and economic élites in the west. (In the late 1980s the then Prime Minister, Margaret Thatcher, directed tax-payers' money into building the much criticised Pergau Dam in Malaysia in return for that country buying arms from UK companies.) Yet we never see anyone involved in the dam project higher than Markham and never get any sense of the wider political and economic determinants at work. And yet the dam is supposed to symbolise the thoughtless destruction of ecosystems by capitalist modernisation. The destruction of the dam at the end unites father and son, so clearly the father/son relationship and the dam are intrinsically connected, yet the dam seems to exist outside any specific socio-historical forces: they are not, at least, present in the film.

The film's naïve belief that its engagement with the subject matter need not require any modification in the long history of the west representing the rest is symptomatically present in its deployment of the character of Werner. He is a photographic journalist sent by his editor to cover Markham's search for his son. Werner's role in the film is entirely plot driven. He functions to introduce us to the Markhams after the ten-year hiatus between the initial abduction and the rest of the film; and in his trip with Markham into the jungle, he works to help the spectator identify fully and uncritically with Markham, since Werner is a sneering cynic, totally untuned to the natural environment. Werner is an implausible character, with little interest in his assignment; he is more like a hack journalist and so a very peculiar choice to cover such a difficult job. Certainly and intriguingly, Werner bears little resemblance to Maureen Bisilliat, the photographer who has covered the Xingu Indians. Dedicated and protective towards the Indians, Boorman used her to make contact with and meet the Amazonian tribe. Now a Third Cinema film might have used the character of Werner in a more complex and self-reflexive way. He could have been used to raise precisely the whole question of the techniques of representation, how the west has framed the rest. Yet this would have necessitated a degree of self-awareness which *The Emerald Forest* cannot contemplate.

JORGE SANJINÉS AND THE UKAMAU GROUP

What blocks Boorman's development as an 'artist' is precisely his Second Cinema conception of himself of what it means to be an artist. Sanjinés, writing as part of the Ukamau group, which has filmed the Andean Indian culture of Bolivia for many years, writes scathingly about the élitism and individualism that underpins the concept of the artist. It is indeed part of the bourgeois ideology which it appears to disdain. One function of the notion of artistic genius is to separate the people from getting involved in cultural production. For this reason, the auteur can be easily grafted onto the hierarchical mode of production of First Cinema, with its contempt for internal democracy and accountability to external sources (except of course when those external sources happen to be estab- lished institutions, like the military, whose property is borrowed in exchange for free and positive public relations).

In making *The Emerald Forest*, Boorman decided not to use tribal Indians. 'Training them to work on a movie would corrupt their way of life and be quite immoral' (1985:73). Certainly this is true if one is working within a First or Second Cinema mode of production but it is not true of film *per se*. What this does is close off any moral pos- sibility of subjecting the film to pressure and input from those whose lives it represents. Sanjinés argues that only by integrating the subject people into the 'creative process' can the artist/art purge itself of bourgeois ideology (1997:62).

Furthermore, when a screenwriter shifts from writing a film about the subject to becoming the 'expressive vehicle' of the subject (the oppressed) this changes the form as well as the content of film. Sanjinés argues that stories that resonate a collective meaning are more likely to be made via a process of collective production (1997:63). He is critical of the Ukamau group's own early film *Blood of the Condor* (1969) because 'our relationship to the peasant actors was still a vertical one' (1997:64). Discussing the question of form, Sanjinés stresses the importance of the long shot in their work. Here he sounds, superficially, a bit like the liberal French film critic André Bazin when he suggests that the close-up imposes the 'viewpoint of the filmmaker, his own interpretation of reality on the viewers' (1997:65). However, Sanjinés does not primarily advocate the long shot because it preserves the rich ambiguity and unity of the scene, as Bazin argued, but because the long shot facilitates the emergence of representation of the collective. This stylistic choice was determined by the peasants and their mode of life.

> Their way of living is not individualistic. They understand reality as the complex integration of everything and everyone... The individualist exists alone and above everything and everyone; the Indian, on the other hand, exists solely in interaction with everything and everyone...I remember an interview we recently filmed where a peasant was demanding the presence of his *companeros* from the community so that he could feel confident and comfortable about what he was saying. Exactly the reverse would happen with an ordinary citizen, who would want to be alone in order to feel secure! (Sanjinés, 1997:66)

Compare this attitude with Boorman's. Apart from the use of subtitles for the Indians (reasonably brave within First Cinema), he never considers whether the form/language of the film has to be adapted to the subject matter. The only time he writes about techniques is in terms of technical difficulties, such as shooting in the jungle or using special effects. The point is not that everyone should follow Sanjinés's model and use the long shot more, but that Sanjinés bothers to think about the relationship between form and content, whereas Boorman, an aspirant Second Cinema director working with little room for manoeuvre within First Cinema, must simply impose the classical model onto the subject matter.

GUERRILLA CINEMA

Third Cinema is sometimes and erroneously made synonymous with what Solanas and Getino termed a 'guerrilla cinema' (1997). This term implies two distinct meanings. A guerrilla cinema could be a cinema that at the level of the text concerns itself with *representations* of guerilla warfare. When the notion of Third Cinema was being formulated in the 1960s and early 1970s, a lot of revolutionary activity, in Latin America especially, was based around armed groups, working in numerous small but connected units, with varying degrees of support in rural areas especially, but also in urban centres as well. The 1959 Cuban revolution was spearheaded by a successful guerrilla struggle and was seen by many as a model of radical political activity (Anderson, 1997). *The Battle of Algiers* would be an example of this kind of cinema, since it focuses on the guerrilla struggles of the Algerian FLN.

However, we may also use the term 'guerrilla cinema' to indicate the conditions of production in which filmmaking was undertaken. When filmmakers are working in conditions of political danger and state authoritarianism, when their work may be seized, censored or when they themselves might be imprisoned, the only way they can film is by using secrecy and subterfuge. In this sense their conditions of work are analogous to the guerrilla: 'In this long war, with the camera as our rifle, we do in fact move into guerrilla activity. This is why the work of a *film-guerrilla* group is governed by strict disciplinary norms as to both work methods and security' (Solanas and Getino, 1997:49).

It should be clear though that Third Cinema cannot be restricted to this definition. The need for Third Cinema does not disappear just because military dictatorships have been replaced by some sort of representative democracy. The world over has seen representative democracy as an effective means of expressing popular will shrivel as the awesome power of capital over social production and reproduction expands (Mèszàros, 1995:673–738). Equally, in those circumstances where revolutionaries successfully acquire *political* power, Third Cinema is a crucial medium through which all the issues involved in extending the revolution into everyday *social* life may be explored. Because guerrilla cinema was important during the initial formulation of Third Cinema due to the political conditions under which filmmakers in Argentina, Bolivia and Chile were operating, there has been a tendency to equate the two cinemas. More sensibly, we must see guerrilla cinema as one strand within Third Cinema; it is not Third Cinema *per se*.

A classic example of guerrilla cinema can be found in the documentary short *Inside Pinochet's Prisons*. After the 1973 coup in Chile, led by General Pinochet, socialists, leftists, sympathisers and others were rounded up in their thousands and detained in over 150 prison camps. There they awaited torture, execution or imprisonment. It was into this situation of fascist dictatorship that an East German communist film group entered Chile on western passports and got access to some of the prisons under the pretence that they were making an anti-communist, pro-Pinochet film. Thus the only thing separating the people behind the camera from the fate of the prisoners they interview is this subterfuge about their real identity and purpose.

Inside Pinochet's Prisons is a simple but surprisingly lyrical film for a documentary report. It includes snippets from an interview with Pinochet. The film reiterates a moment prior to the start of the interview: Pinochet is settling into his chair, dressed in an immaculate white military suit; he is preening himself. A formal strategy such as repetition foregrounds authorial comment very clearly. For the filmmakers do not pretend to aspire to objectivity or neutrality. The voice-over notes the irony of Pinochet, the 'anti-communist' lamenting on camera how difficult it is to wipe out communism, while he is talking...to communists!

With Pinochet's approval, the filmmakers fly north and visit two prisons. What is interesting about this film and what makes it, as a text, an example of Third Cinema, is the importance it attaches to culture. The soundtrack uses songs, music and poetry, the latter taking the form of a poem by the narrator directed to Chile's political prisoners. Fernando Birri has described Latin American cinema as being characterised by a 'poetics of the transformation of reality' (1997b:96). What Birri means by this I think is that cinema, like poetry, must immerse itself in and generate a cultural energy and creativity if it is to act as a model and conductor of the kinds of energies required to transform the world beyond the screening of the film. The notion of a poetics of cinema is central to the emphasis Birri places on 'the need to expand our horizons' (1997b:96). A film that is worthy but dull and unimaginative is a film that will fail to inspire, fail to motivate, fail to articulate the cultural resources which the exploited must draw on if they are to resist the agenda of capital.

Inside Pinochet's Prisons not only mobilises culture on its soundtrack, it is highly sensitive to the way culture becomes a site of political struggle within the regime of the prisons. At Chacabuco prison the prisoners have the opportunity to give a church service. No doubt the military authorities imagined that Christianity represented *their* values and that the prisoners were undergoing a kind of re-education programme by participating in the service. But, as the narrator notes, the service affords the opportunity for meeting and 'collective expression'. Furthermore, the discourse of Christianity itself is transformed in the mouths of socialists. 'They sang a story of the Passion of Christ, transformed here into a key message: the suffering and bravery of the good man.' The soloist, we learn, is the doctor who was in charge of childcare in the Allende government overthrown by the coup.

The documentary concludes emphatically on this question of culture and all that this word implies: identity, beliefs, values. At another prison, Pisagua, the authorities make the prisoners sing the national anthem.

> Pure is your blue sky Chile
> Pure too is the breeze that crosses you
> And your fields of embroidered flowers
> Are the happy image of Eden
> Magestic the white mountain
> That God gave you as a bastion.

It is a typically conservative anthem, one in which the country is evacuated of the real people and real difficulties and replaced with a banal imagery of nature merging with national harmony, sanctioned by God and, with the mountains as a 'bastion', just a hint of rivalry and aggression to others. The imposition of this song on the prisoners is of course deeply political but, as the narrator notes, its meaning undergoes a transformation: 'the song has become a hymn of resistance'.

HISTORICITY

One of Marx's most recurrent strategies of critique in his readings of bourgeois political economists was to show how these writers tried to freeze history so as to present the capital system as the 'end of history', the summit to which humanity can climb and beyond which it would be folly or madness to go. Marx writes:

> Political economy starts with the fact of private property; it does not explain it to us...Political economy throws no light on the cause of the division between labour and capital, and between capital and land. When, for example, it defines the relationship of wages to profit, it takes the interest of the capitalist to be the ultimate cause, i.e., it takes for granted what it is supposed to explain. (quoted in Reiss, 1997:93–4)

Mèszàros finds a similar strategy among economists even today:

> The defenders of capital cannot acknowledge the historical character and limits of the established mode and structures of

reproductive mediation. In their eagerness to eternalise the capital system as one to which there can be no alternative, they try to characterise a highly specific mode of socioeconomic interchange, based on the historically constituted rule of capital, as if it was in its substance timeless and possessed an absolutely unquestionable, universal validity. (Mèszàros, 1995:136–7)

This eternalisation of capital is not restricted to the economists but is deeply embedded into the general culture. Eternalisation of the present means that when history gets represented, what is actually happening is that a historically determined society (dominated by capital) is simply projecting itself *back* into the past. By finding itself in the past, the present reassures itself that it was always meant to be and that there will be no other alternatives or paths for humankind, for how can there be when society as it is constituted can find images of itself throughout time?

It is not that a historical drama cannot show change – indeed the classical narrative is predicated precisely on things changing; the key question is *how* and *why* there is change. Within western capitalism what has been represented as the key agent of history is the individual. We have already seen that Third Cinema offers a critique of the individualistic conception of the artist. We must now see how Third Cinema theory and practice offers a critique of and alternative to historiography (whether academic or mass media representations) premised on the individual. An account of historical change which starts from and ends with the individual is problematic because it is unable to show how the individual is formed within a broader set of social relationships and how they develop in conjunction with those relationships.

AMISTAD

Steven Spielberg's 1997 film is set in the mid-nineteenth century and concerns the fate of black slaves who capture the ship they are being transported on (the *Amistad*). Although they kill the crew, the slave owner persuades them that he will navigate them back to Africa but, instead, he sets sail for America. When the ship is captured by the American navy, the slaves are thrown in jail while various parties squabble over the question of to whom do the blacks belong. Their case is taken up by the abolitionists who are pressing for slavery to be abolished in the American South. Their fate thus becomes tied up with American internal politics and a weak President seeking re-election who requires the support of the Southern slave states.

The film does have some strengths. It certainly presents the slave trade in all its brutality. The flashback scene in which Cinque, the main black slave character, recalls the journey on the *Amistad* prior to the revolt, shows graphically what happens when human beings are treated like cattle, cargo or any other commodity. When for example the slave owners realise that they do not have enough food provision for the journey, they simply chain 50 slaves together, tie rocks to them and dump them overboard. The film foregrounds the conception of the slaves as commodities, as the property of others, via the trial process, where various parties claim the blacks as 'belonging' to them.

The film's critique of this notion involves offering instead the idea of human rights. Yet while human rights are important in any context where they are being denied, the liberal conception of human rights is severely limited. Marx criticised its view of liberty because it equated freedom with the right to own private property. Marx writes: 'None of the so-called rights of man, therefore, go beyond egoistic man...that is an individual withdrawn into himself, into the confines of his private interests and private caprice, and separated from the community' (Reiss, 1997:87).

Now, what Marx was concerned with here is not private property *per se* (a television set, for example) but *productive* property which exploits labour: factories, offices, land, capital, and so on. Within the liberal conception of human rights, there is no conflict between this property and human freedom. Thus for the film the struggle against slavery is the final struggle against the frustration of the rights of man. Thus *wage-slavery*, the transformation of *labour power* into a commodity, the coercion and 'ownership' involved in selling labour to capital (or being discarded by capital) cannot be admitted within the narrative of the film.

The agent of historical change within *Amistad* is the realisation *by individuals* of the fundamental human rights of others. It is a story in which indifference turns to a commitment to liberty, a story where strangers become friends, and where each important individual realises their essential goodness, their essential strengths, and throws off the cynicism of their professions (as lawyers or politi-cians) and their own *private* weaknesses. Thus Roger Baldwin initially takes the case of the black slaves and sees it essentially as a 'property question'. If he can prove that the slaves do not belong to anyone (that they were not born slaves and that they came from Africa) then the legitimate rights of property do not in this case apply. The abolitionists who hire him make it clear that they do not believe this is the proper way of conceiving the question. Although Baldwin is successful in proving that the slaves were taken illegally from a British protectorate (there is, of course, no criticism of British or any other colonialism in the film) where the slave trade is banned, the case is moved to the court of appeal by the President, anxious about Southern votes. At this point, mysteriously, Baldwin undergoes a transformation and, exchanging glances with Cinque, bonds with him and the cause of the slaves at what the film evidently feels is the more appropriate profound level of human rights.

A similar transformation is undergone by the character of John Quincy Adams, an ex-President, lawyer and now elderly member of the House of Representatives. Initially approached by the abolitionists to represent the slaves, he rebuffs them outright. Later, after the first trial is moved to the court of appeal, the black abolitionist Joadson (Morgan Freeman) approaches Adams once again, asking for help. Adams again rebuffs him, but melts a little. As Joadson is leaving, Adams abruptly changes his mind and begins to ask questions about the case and then proffers his advice. After the case is won a second time by Baldwin, the President moves the case up to the Supreme Court, loaded, we are told, with judges from the South, who themselves own slaves. Once again Adams is approached and now he is ready to commit himself to the case fully. The film makes sure that we know that he is mocked by other politicians as an eccentric has-been. Thus, in his own way, he too, like the young Baldwin, is a 'little man' with something to prove and greater powers to overcome. The film presents Adams winning the case through his great rhetorical power (emphasised throughout the film) where he single-handedly rescues the progressive values of the American revolution in a scene constructed to give maximum power to a 'virtuoso' performance by Anthony Hopkins.

Amistad presents history as the outcome of the decisions and actions taken by individuals divorced from any larger social context. Why do individuals do the things they do? Why do they have the beliefs and values they have? How does change come about? In *Amistad* change comes about when individuals realise what is already, as far as the film is concerned, self-evident: that people should not be slaves. Thus the film projects back into the past its own bourgeois liberal values. Typically, then, the only social problem which the film troubles to find is slavery, which, once abolished, will allow society to unfold into the 'paradise' of the present social order. The film even manages to find an America devoid of the racism which marks it to this day. We must turn now to another way of thinking historically.

HISTORY, HEGEL AND MARX

The word 'dialectics' is actually very old (it can be traced back to ancient Greece) and it has had different nuances of meaning. Raymond Williams notes that within medieval Europe the term referred to the 'art of discussion and debate' (Williams, 1988:106). In other words, it referred to the clash of opinions and ideas and the advancement of knowledge through a process of disputation. The concept of dialectics within history was given a decisive role by the German philosopher G. W. Hegel (1770–1831). Hegel argued that history was characterised by the clash between incompatible forces straining against each other and manifesting themselves in rival intellectual ideas, moral attitudes and movements (Berlin, 1963:55). Hegel takes that sense of the dialectic as a dispute, as a dialogue of conflicting ideas and applies it to the whole of human history. This notion of struggle and tension provides the dynamic principle that is required to account for change within history. History is the outcome of interacting forces which are modified and changed by their conflictual relations. In Hegel's era the key conflicts and changes revolved around the democratic and republican ideas unleashed by the French Revolution (with which Hegel aligned himself) and the feudal, monarchist past.

The young Marx, studying at the University of Berlin, was profoundly influenced by this vision of historical change. However, there was one major limitation with Hegel's conception. Hegel saw history as the outcome of conflicting ideas, values and beliefs. Hegel advocated a struggle for a higher consciousness in which those ideas which were the most rational (as against, for example, the superstitions promoted by the Church, which had provided monarchies everywhere with some legitimation) should/would become concretised in institutional forms, such as the state. Hegel's philosophy was 'idealist' – that is to say, history was seen as the outcome of the development of the most advanced, rational ideas.

Marx however developed a 'materialist' dialectic. Here, ideas, values, beliefs are generated as part of such physical, material forces as socioeconomic relationships. These relationships are conflictual (for example, the conflict between capital and labour) and so the ideas, values and beliefs which people have are conflictual. But more than that, the notion of the dialectic (and this was present in Hegel's work as well) involves not just conflicts *between* different and opposed forces, but also *internal* conflicts or contradictions *within* them (Rees, 1998:50–51). Thus labour and capital are internally contradictory: they each produce their own negation (labour produces that which will exploit it – capital, and capital produces the social force which represents its own antithesis – wage-labour, the collective majority). Similarly, ideas, values and beliefs are internally contradictory, providing their own response or mediation of the conflicts between capital and labour. This way of thinking about history requires us to *locate* the actions and beliefs of individuals in their wider socioeconomic context and to understand change as something that is brought about not by individuals realising a 'timeless' principle but by individuals and collectives operating within conflictual and contradictory relationships that shape what can be thought and what can be done at any particular point in time and space.

THE LAST SUPPER

It is worth comparing *Amistad* with the Cuban film *The Last Supper* (1976) by Tomás Gutiérrez Alea (whose theoretical work we will look at in the last chapter). The film is set in a Havana sugar mill, worked by black slave labour, in the late eighteenth century. The film develops the ideas of a Marxist historiography discussed above. The film begins with the doors of the slaves' sleeping quarters being hurled open. The overseer, Don Manuel (himself a mulatto) is furious because one of the slaves, Sebastian, has escaped. Where *Amistad* opens with a huge close-up of Cinque (underlining the importance of individuals as the sole explanatory force), *The Last Supper* begins with the effects of an escape and will explore it as a symptom of a much bigger problem for the sugar mill. The Count who owns the mill returns after a short absence and is greeted by the priest and attended to by his black house slaves. For the first half of the film, the blacks are virtually silent and speak only when spoken to by the whites. They occupy the background of the action: but the film is not unconsciously reproducing a racist dramaturgy. A slight pan here follows a female slave as she walks across the corridor, another scene shows the slaves attending to the bath of the Count. The film is fully aware that their silent labours support everything and call into question the values and beliefs of the whites. Gradually, though, the blacks will move from the background to the foreground, from passivity to revolt.

The priest complains to the Count how hard it is teaching Christian doctrine to the blacks when they are not allowed to come to Church by the overseer and when the overseer himself behaves in such un-Christian ways as getting drunk. The Count meanwhile is looking for moral and spiritual guidance and has a special plan for the black slaves in regard to teaching them Christianity. However, he refuses to condemn the overseer, noting merely that he has a difficult job. We have here then a major contradiction between his professed faith and the economic necessity to exploit slave labour. Later he conveys to Don Manuel the priest's complaint. Don Manuel counters that 'production' means that he would have to whip the slaves harder during the week if he gives them Sundays off on a regular basis. The Count becomes bad tempered. He does not want to know *these* details, he just wants them in Church more regularly. Behind him, background right, another slave stands silent.

The Count then goes to the sugar mill where we meet Don Gaspar, who is in charge of the mill. Don Gaspar explains to the Count his latest technical innovations and initiatives to refine the sugar. This triggers a debate between Gaspar, a man of science, and the priest about where the secrets of these new techniques comes from. The film suggests that the motive for these innovations comes from the need to expand production. The Count tells Gaspar that he has been in negotiations with an English firm to buy a new press and Gaspar agrees that this will increase production still further. However, he warns the Count that this will mean more slave labour being brought onto the plantation. The Count shrugs nonchalantly but Gaspar points out (having seen a rebellion on another plantation) that eventually there will be many more blacks than whites. So here we have another contradiction: this time, between expanding production and maintaining the socioeconomic order of the plantation. The story then has opened with the social order already in process, undergoing change. At this point, Sebastian – this symptom of growing turbulence – appears, having been caught. Don Manuel cuts off his ear and feeds it to the dogs.

The title of the film refers of course to Christ's last supper with his disciples, where he tried to prepare them for his death and impart his final teachings. In the film, the Count recreates the last supper on Palm Sunday, inviting twelve blacks from the plantation, including Sebastian, to eat with him where he casts himself in the role of Christ the teacher. The priest prepares the slaves for this event with a sermon. He tells them what a utopia Heaven is, a place of equality, peace and plenty. Yet only the pure go there and the pure are precisely those who have accepted the precise opposite on earth: inequality, poverty and pain.

The supper itself is a very subtle process in which the consciousness of the slaves undergoes certain changes, although not in the Christian direction hoped for by the Count. At first the slaves, bemused by the whole event, hardly dare to talk. Gradually, though, they start speaking with the Count. Some play the black fool, hoping to ingratiate themselves with him, others directly ask for favours, others still have a strong sense of self-respect, such as Bangoche, who was a king in Africa. Songs are sung, stories are told, the nature of freedom is discussed. The stories which the blacks tell are rooted in a pragmatic recognition and acceptance of the harsh realities of life. By contrast, the stories which the Count tells are idealistic morality tales that teach acceptance of the *status quo* as the price to be paid in order to ascend to Heaven. The blacks however start to challenge the morality of necessary suffering; they begin to engage in debate. Their resentment towards the overseer bubbles up and they ask why, if there is no overseer in Heaven, should there be one on Earth. At this stage, as they are debating with the Count, they are directing their grievances at the overseer, not the Count who employs him. However, as the evening wears on, everyone, including the Count, gets very drunk. One of the slaves starts throwing bits of food at the Count. The Count subsequently falls asleep. Sebastian then tells a story about how it came to pass that two gods, Truth and Lie, swapped heads, so that to this day, Lie has the body of Truth and vice-versa. This story shakes the slaves and they begin to debate whether the master himself is evil, whether he speaks the truth or lies. The key question for the slaves boils down to something very practical and immediate: whether, as the master promised, they will get a day off work on Good Friday.

Good Friday comes but there is no rest for the slaves. While the slaves protest to Don Manuel that the master has said there would be no work, Don Manuel knows that the Count has told him that 'production' is his responsibility. Whereas a First Cinema film would be tempted to rest the blame for subsequent events on an over-zealous individual, *The Last Supper* makes it clear that the overseer's actions are a product of the economic necessities impinging on the mill. Thus when the Father runs to the Count to complain, the Count dismisses him and sides with his economic interests. Don Manuel's action of course proves to be the last straw and so the slaves revolt, taking him prisoner. Thinking that the Count can be appealed to to dispense justice, the slaves send a delegation to negotiate. He, however, now puts aside all interest in Christian teachings and responds ferociously. Realising that reconciliation is impossible, the slaves burn large parts of the mill and Sebastian kills Don Manuel.

The final part of the film is concerned with the hunt for the escaped slaves. The ones who took the lead, it seems, were those who sat around the table with the Count. By Easter Sunday, there are eleven heads on pikes. Sebastian is the only one not to be caught. The final shot of the film sees him on the run. History is not finished, the struggle is not over.

The Last Supper is a film about the contradiction between religion and capital, even as the Church accommodates itself to business and in return lends some ideological legitimation to the new ruling class, just as it did during the feudal era. The Count is here a typical figure (in the Lukácsian sense): both aspiring to be a devout Christian while also being the owner of a capitalist business. He embodies the contradictions of the age. It is also a film about the processes by which the exploited become conscious of their condition and begin to question the social order and it explores the circumstances under which that questioning may turn into open revolt.

A MARXIST DEFINITION OF TRAGEDY

The Last Supper is similar to Ousmane Sembene's film *Camp de Thiaroye* (1987). Set at the end of the Second World War, the film explores the process by which a group of African soldiers who have fought as part of the French colonial army are now on the cusp of a politicised response to French racism. The final straw comes when the French try to cheat the Africans of their proper back-pay. In answer to their revolt, the French destroy them and their base camp using tanks and machine guns. As with *The Last Supper*, the revolt is unsuccessful and it is brutally crushed. Aristotelian definitions of tragedy in particular have often been read as having a conservative effect by reminding the audience of the high cost of necessarily (within tragedy) unsuccessful attempts to challenge authority (Drakakis, 1992:1–44). However, within Third Cinema the tragedy works rather differently. These films are tragedies because the revolts are historically premature; they are premature anticipations of the later struggles that *will succeed* but which can only come at the expense of preceding generations sacrificing their lives. This sacrifice lays down the first markers that capitalism and colonialism are historically relative and that the rule of the exploiters will be contested by the exploited. But these first, tentative, embryonic struggles, so small, so isolated, will fail. The tragedy lies in the discrepancy between the necessity to revolt, to reaffirm their identity and dignity, and the historical conditions which give the dominant classes an overwhelming advantage. The massacre at the end of *Camp de Thiaroye* is rather like the shooting of the striking workers in Eisenstein's *Strike* (1924). The viewer is not drawn into the action to experience it cathartically, but instead views events from a distance; angrily but with a measure of dispassion so that the historical conclusions can be drawn. *The Last Supper* opts for another strategy. It remains true to the tragic consequences of this historically premature revolt but retains, in the figure of Sebastian, a symbolic figure of freedom and independence: for surely, we are not meant to read his escape in literal terms. Sebastian is running towards the future.

POLITICISATION AND COMMITMENT

The Greek director Costa Gavras was largely responsible for launching and popularising a new genre in the late 1960s. The background to this was the worldwide political and social upheavals of the period (Hill, 1997:131). Unsurprisingly, this generated a debate concerning the political role of film in a context of social unrest. Gavras is often credited with mapping out one option: the political thriller. This involved taking the established conventions of such entertainment forms as the thriller, the film noir, the detective genre and injecting into these films a new type of story content designed to raise political questions. The Gavras film *Z* (1968), for example, was based on a true story about the assassination of a Greek MP and the subsequent cover-up by the authorities. The film explored the Greek state, its secret machinations, unaccountability and its subordination to American foreign policy aims. Hollywood directors appropriated this form in such films as *The Parallax View* (Alan J. Pakula, 1974), *Three Days of the Condor* (Sydney Pollack, 1975) and *All the President's Men* (Alan J. Pakula, 1976). In some films it is the role of private corporations and big business which is the site of conspiracy; in others, it is the state, or a mixture of the two. Contemporary examples of the genre include *Enemy of the State* (Tony Scott, 1998) and the sci-fi political hybrid *The X-Files* (Rob Bowman, 1998). The question, from a Third Cinema perspective, is whether the forms adopted have been sufficiently transformed to be able to represent the complexities of the social order. Summarising the reservations that a number of critics have had about the form, John Hill asks whether the genre does not 'encourage explanations of social realities in individual and psychological terms, rather than economic and political ones'. The broader issues raised by the conspiracy being investigated tend to be deflected into 'interpersonal relations' (Hill, 1997:132).

These problems are very evident in Gavras's 1981 Hollywood-produced film *Missing*, starring Jack Lemmon and Sissy Spacek. The films draws on the star images of these actors: Lemmon as the conservative, white-collar, middle management type; Spacek, the hippy-dippy outsider type. Unlike Pontecorvo's *Burn*, the film does not deconstruct the star system and our habitual modes of identification but sets up an initial tension between these conflicting types before they are, in classic fashion, gradually drawn together in the course of their investigation. Thus the interpersonal relations are foregrounded rather than the wider social and political issues.

Based on a true story, the film is set in Chile, 1973. It is about the disappearance of a young American, Charles Horman, shortly after the coup. Lemmon plays Charles's father and Spacek his wife, Beth. Horman senior arrives in Santiago full of conservative, middle-America complacency, barely understanding the coup or the implications it might have for his disappeared son. Gradually he and the spectator learn of the complicity of the American CIA and military in the coup as senior officials mislead and frustrate Horman's search.

The film does have the merit of identifying the imperialist quality of American foreign policy and even links it to the protection of business interests. In this way at least, it avoids the trap of suggesting that the problem uncovered is the fault of a few atypical individuals (one of the limitations of *Enemy of the State*). Yet *Missing* makes its political point in the most depoliticised way.

The relationship between Horman and Beth is also used as a way of telling us about the relationship between Charlie and his father. Although from Horman's conservative perspective Beth and Charlie appear to be 'radicals', it becomes clear that the tension between Charlie and his father was, in that classic narrative structure, generational rather than political. The film emphasises the innocent, almost naïve quality of Beth and Charlie (their penchant for children's toys, stories and pictures). The implication is that their story is tragic precisely because they were not really 'mixed up' in the politics of Chilean society. If they had been, perhaps Charlie would have deserved his fate. Intrinsic to this presentation of two innocents is the fact that Charlie and Beth are living an expatriate life that is isolated from the wider events of the society around them.

In Chile in the early 1970s there were few Chileans who were politically innocent: everyone, whether left, right or in-between, knew they were living through intensely politicised times. Thus the weaknesses of the political thriller are redoubled when we factor in the geo-cultural issue that this is a Hollywood product telling a story set in Chile but radically marginalising the Chileans. This is highlighted in the scene in which Beth and Horman are watching an 8mm film of a barbecue party. We see Charlie and a friend *posing* as Chilean peasants where one tries to persuade the other of the virtues of the revolution using a simple dim-witted discourse. Just as the figure of Werner in *The Emerald Forest* signifies the film's inability to subject its own modes of representation to any critique or reflection, so this muted, self-reflexive moment in *Missing* merely highlights its problematic inability to represent the other with any complexity, history or cultural specificity. The Chilean revolution was certainly not made by dim-wits, nor was it primarily a *peasant* revolution, although peasants were certainly an important constituency of the oppressed. Primarily, though, the revolution was made by highly politicised, class-conscious workers.

REVOLUTION AND THIRD CINEMA

I have suggested that if Third Cinema is to retain its critical capacities, it cannot simply align itself to a progressive government, however that is defined. We have seen in Sembene's *Xala* that the rise to power of black nationalist leaders hardly led to any improvement in the lives of ordinary blacks after the end of colonial rule. Third Cinema must align itself to the more profound *social* transformations that must follow the acquiring of political power. Nowhere is this more evident than the example of Chile, which ought to be seared on the memory of the left. When Salvador Allende came to power in 1970, it was as the head of Popular Unity, a coalition of left-wing parties, of which the Socialist Party and the Communist Party were the largest. Allende was hailed as the first democratically elected Marxist and Chile was seen internationally as a model for achieving socialism through the institutions and organisations that had been developed within capitalism. Except that capital, both nationally and internationally, was quite prepared (as it was in Europe in the 1920s and 1930s) to suspend parliamentary democracy and use the fascist jackboot to break the organisations of labour and progressives generally. The journalist Neal Ascherson recalls flying into Chile shortly after the coup:

> A German on the plane, representing Mercedes Benz, assured me: 'Now the economy will surge up again. They told me on the phone the factory is still working; the generals have abolished the five-day week and you can sack any worker who comes in after 8.30 in the morning.' (Ascherson, 1998:9)

Although Allende did his best to reassure the dominant classes that he would work within the rules and constitution of bourgeois Chilean democracy, those rules and the constitution were shattered by the dominant class because the main power struggle, the main point of contention, the seismic rift within Chilean society, was taking place *outside* parliament, between capital and labour. Every time capital attempted to undermine Popular Unity by sabotaging the economy with investment strikes, shutting down factories, seizing up the transport network by locking up lorries, the key, fundamental question of ownership and control over productive resources was posed to labour. And labour began to respond in kind, by asserting its rights, its strengths, its own modes of collective,

democratic control. Workers' committees and community organisations began to emerge, which started to organise life from the
bottom up. Here, in embryonic form, was that broader, more
profound transformation of social life that Third Cinema is a
component of and a conduit for its re-presentation.

THE BATTLE OF CHILE

We are immensely fortunate to have in Patricio Guzman's documentary film *The Battle of Chile* (shot during 1973, but edited over
the next three years in Cuba) a record of this social transformation,
this embryo of an alternative future, before it was snuffed out by the
generals and the economic interests they represent. The film
immerses itself in the ongoing revolution; in the debates, arguments,
aspirations of a people who are changing the world around them
and themselves. The documentary form has long been associated
with the voice of specialists, professionals and authority figures. It
tends to draw ordinary people into its frame of reference only when
they are victims of some social or political violence or, alternatively,
as entertainment, the depoliticised presentation of everyday life. The
opportunity that is opened up when everyday life becomes extraordinary and intensely political is the space into which *The Battle of
Chile* jumps.

The documentary explores the intensifying class struggle within
Chile in 1973, the last year of Allende's government before the *coup
d'état*. Despite the fact that here was a government which proclaimed
itself to be 'of the people', *The Battle of Chile* does not view events
from the perspective of the government. Instead it explores the space
between Allende's government and the working class. Despite the
enormous and evident respect and affection with which Allende was
held by working people, the film also reveals the impatience and
frustration they increasingly felt towards the government. Two key
issues were driving the working class to the left of the Allende
government: the question of arming the people and the question of
'popular power'.

Part Two of *The Battle of Chile* opens with the aborted military
coup of June 1973 which is put down by troops loyal to the
government. This opening sequence is dominated by the voice-over
narrator who describes how a single regiment attacks the
government headquarters, the La Moneda palace where Allende will

later die in the September coup. In June, though, the army is divided and the rebel troops are isolated. The voice-over describes the events as they unfold. There is street fighting between the rebel troops and troops loyal to the government. Gradually the uprising is defeated and crowds gather outside the La Moneda palace. Various military and government officials are trying to disperse the crowd and the voice-over adopts the sort of confidence in offialdom which is typical of the conventional documentary form. 'José Tohá,' we are told, 'Minister of Defence, tries to instil calm in the face of possible danger. He is assisted in this task by General Pickering.' There is a pronounced dissonance between this voice-over's investment in authority figures and the chants of the crowd, such as: 'Fight and create popular power.'

Then as the events of the summer unfold the film increasingly commits itself to giving representation to the sounds and images of the people. A group of women discuss the necessity of arming the people so that they can protect and extend the gains that the government has made, even as the army begins a series of provocative raids on working-class districts and factories, under the pretext of searching for arms: the very thing which they do not have. Again and again, demonstrators call on the government to give them arms, to create a people's militia. Allende's government, however, remains absolutely wedded to the bourgeois constitution which makes it dependent on the official army, staffed by middle-class officers committed to defend the private property relations that the working class were challenging both ideologically and in practice.

This is the second key division between Allende's government and the working class: again and again, in meetings, debates and demonstrations, we see the call go up for 'popular power'. The working class had taken over many industries, they had set up organs for grass roots control both in the factories and in the neighbourhoods. This is the classic revolutionary situation of dual power: where the old forms of political and economic power are still in place but are increasingly being challenged by new emergent, still embryonic socialist forms of economic and political power. The Allende government, however, remained wedded to the old forms of power and were ambivalent in their attitudes towards the newly emergent organs of workers' control.

There is a scene in *The Battle of Chile* that illustrates these tensions. In fact it is rather reminiscent of the key scene in Ken Loach's *Land and Freedom* (1995) where a village just liberated from the fascists by the POUM (Workers Marxist Unity Party) debate whether or not to collectivise all the land or just some of it. One of the members of the POUM who (significantly enough) later leaves and joins the Communist Party argues for moderation, suggesting that radical collectivisation will harm the legality of the Republican government and damage Spain's relations with foreign capitalist powers whose assistance the government might need.

In *The Battle of Chile*, almost exactly the same argument is put by a trade union official at a meeting called to discuss what is to happen to the industries currently in the hands of the workers. The delegate, like the fictional character in *Land and Freedom*, worries that the expropriation of Swiss capital by the workers might damage Chile's position with the Club of Paris, of which Switzerland is a member, who handle the national debt. As with the character in *Land and Freedom*, the trade union official also worries that such radicalism might damage the legality of the Allende government. The counter-argument is put by a worker from the floor, who speaks with a passion, eloquence and perceptiveness which would undoubtedly be left on the cutting-room floor of a mainstream news organisation. He argues that there is little point in building up the organisations of popular power if the trade union officials, government officials and the President do not believe in or have faith in working class, bottom-up democracy. He identifies how they are all struggling with the problem of bureaucracy, the top-down dissemination of power and the division of labour which leaves politics and decision-making in the hands of 'specialists'. His speech receives huge applause from the floor and suggests how limited are the ambitions of those who cannot contemplate new forms of social, economic and political power.

The Battle of Chile is a partisan documentary. It does not aspire to understand 'both sides' in the antagonistic struggle between capital and labour. There can be no middle position in this conflict. To adopt a mid-way point between capital and labour is to deny their fundamental antagonism which in turn means that such a mid-way position is not really 'balanced' but is in actuality operating within the horizon of capital which must also deny a fundamental conflict of interest between itself and the source of its own existence: labour power. However, while taking up a position that is committed to labour, *The Battle of Chile* also explores the diversity of positions and debates within the left as to how to progress the revolution. Thus the film demonstrates the fallacy of liberal documentary practice which assumes that political commitment equals dogma and closure.

CULTURAL SPECIFICITY AND POPULAR MEMORY

We have seen that one of the distinctive characteristics of Third Cinema is the importance it attaches to the question of culture. Understanding that culture is the crucial realm in which identity, beliefs and values are forged, Third Cinema intervenes in culture as a site of struggle. One of the modes by which a democratic culture of the masses gets articulated is through popular memory. In an important essay, Teshome Gabriel has explored some of the links between popular memory and Third Cinema. Gabriel notes how popular memory is kept alive in songs, stories, poems and music (hence the importance of these forms for *Inside Pinochet's Prisons*). The oral and unofficial nature of popular memory is crucially important because it circumvents the printed word (newspapers and books) and the educational institutions that disseminate 'official history'.

> Official history tends to arrest the future by means of the past. Historians privilege the written word of the text – it serves as their rule of law. It claims a 'centre' which continuously marginalises others. In this way its ideology inhibits people from constructing their own history or histories. (Gabriel, 1989:53)

In contrast to this top-down history, popular memory does not close off the future (in the way *Amistad* does, for example) by closing off the past. It does not treat the past as fixed and distant, but as protean and relevant to the changing needs of the present, feeding the struggles that have still to be fought, rather than affirming a present in which all struggles have been won (*Amistad*, again). Stories in popular memory are open-ended, adaptable and changing, not fixed and closed. Thus there is an affinity here with the open-ended quality of Third Cinema. Both Third Cinema and popular memory also emphasise a history in which individuals are profoundly connected to the world around them. It is the people and not a few outstanding individuals who make history.

INDOCHINE

I want to explore the dialectics between First and Third Cinema by discussing an example of how First Cinema may mobilise a specific aspect of Third Cinema – oral culture and popular memory – but transform its revolutionary potential into a conservative representation. The French film *Indochine* (Régis Wargnier, 1991) is an epic First Cinema love story set against the French colonial domination of Indochina generally and Vietnam specifically. The film is set during the 1930s, a period of economic crisis in the colonies as much as in Europe. This decade saw the emergence of the Vietnamese Communist Party as the leading organisation in the struggle for national liberation.

The story constructs a love triangle. There is Eliane Devries (Catherine Deneuve), a strong independent woman who presides over a vast rubber plantation. She has a passionate affair with a young naval officer, Le-Guen, who then falls in love with Eliane's adopted Vietnamese daughter, Camille. Eliane's influence within the colonial hierarchy enables her to have Le-Guen sent to a remote outpost on the Gulf of Tonkin. Camille however leaves her comfortable, secure, high-bourgeois existence and sets out to find Le-Guen. She plunges into a country racked by poverty and unrest. Le-Guen meanwhile has found that the French presence in Vietnam has degenerated beyond redemption. The officials in control of the outpost are involved in a slave market whereby workers from the north, driven by desperation and poverty, are sold into slavery to work the plantations in the south. It is here that Camille is swept, caught up in the mass movement of people. Le-Guen and Camille meet and a drama is played out before the watching but passive Vietnamese. Le-Guen leads Camille away from the holding pens and is berated by the French officer in command. Camille, for her part, sees a woman she befriended lying dead in the water. A fight breaks out, a gun spills to the floor, Camille picks it up and shoots the officer. The Vietnamese surge forward in the holding pens and have to be cowed again by the French.

Wanted for murder, the two lovers go on the run. A friend of Camille's, now working for the Communist Party, arranges for them to join a Communist theatre troupe which will take them to China. The troupe tours Vietnam performing revolutionary plays and provoking insurrections against local landlords. Teshome Gabriel detects a 'significant continuity' between the modes of address and reception that popular memory and Third Cinema mobilise. 'This continuity consists of a sharing of responsibility in the construction of the text, where both the film-maker and the spectators play a double role as performers and creators' (1989:62).

Indochine offers us a glimmer of this 'double role' in Third Cinema/popular memory, as the theatre audiences become in turn revolutionary subjects, re-creating the world beyond the performance. The travelling theatre, deeply embedded into Vietnamese popular culture for centuries, is able to avoid the suspicion of the French authorities. Until, that is, the French inspector looking for Camille and Le-Guen identifies the role of the theatre troupes and orders the arrest of all artists in the region. With an ironic sense of cultural struggle, the inspector gives the crackdown the codename Operation Molière (echoing the paratroop commander in *Battle of Algiers*, when he names a crackdown on the strike Operation Champagne).

Camille meanwhile has given birth to a son (the story is being told in flashback by Eliane to Camille's son). Le-Guen however is arrested along with the baby. Here begins the film's most audacious mobilisation of popular memory. Eliane's voice-over tells how the baby, still only a few weeks old, suckled at the breasts of Vietnamese women on the journey back south. We see a woman feeding the baby while the camera pans round to a crowd of people who have come to watch. Eliane tells us: 'Indo-Chinese women nourished you at every stop. That's how the legend began...With you. Countless women said they nourished you, even elderly women, even those who'd never seen you.'

The participation of the masses, whether real or imagined, generates a story, a legend. This popular folklore is then taken up and given further amplification by the theatre troupes. We see the scene at the slave market and the fateful shooting being re-enacted for the Vietnamese peasants. So then: we are asked to believe that a love affair between a white French naval officer and a bourgeois woman assimilated to French culture, not even actively involved in the liberation struggle, can become the hero and heroine of the Vietnamese masses; we are asked to believe that the killing of a single officer at the slave market has propelled them to the front of the struggle; that they would gather round and watch in wonder as the offspring of these two individuals is embraced by and sustained by the collective bosom of the masses, even while their own children are dying from hunger and poverty and disease all around. What this shows is that the dialectics between First, Second and Third Cinema works both ways. Third Cinema may appropriate and transform components of First and Second Cinema to its own cause; but conversely here in *Indochine* popular memory, as a component of Third Cinema, is inverted to valorise two depoliticised romantics from the bourgeoisie.

DISTRIBUTION AND EXHIBITION: CAPITAL AND THE STATE

What makes films like *Missing*, *The Emerald Forest*, *Amistad* and *Indochine* particularly problematic is not just their intrinsic limitations but the conditions of their reception which means that they achieve hugely greater exposure to mass audiences than alternative and contesting stories. The difficulty for radical filmmakers in getting their films to the audience is an enduring, structural and persistent problem. 'This happens', Birri noted:

> and we denounce the fact – not because of the films themselves or our public, but because the films themselves are systematically boycotted by both national and international distributors and exhibitors, who are linked to the anti-national and colonial interests of foreign producers, above all those of North American cinema. (1997a:90–1)

While access to cultural production has become easier with the technological development of cheaper and lighter recording equipment, the means of disseminating cultural products and of gaining access to audiences lies in the domination of distribution and exhibition by monopoly capital. Birri goes on:

> Exhibitors and distributors justify their permanent blocking of nationally produced films by appealing to the spectator's right to choose what films he or she wishes to see. But this free-market sophism omits one small detail: that for an audience to choose a film, it must first be exhibited, which generally does not happen with national films, or does so only in appalling conditions. (1997a:91)

In order to counter this marginalisation, Sanjinés and the Ukamau group toured the Latin American countryside with a portable generator in order to show *Blood of the Condor* in villages without electricity. In periods of large-scale politicisation, the audience for revolutionary cinema expands. Sanjinés gives impressive audience figures for the Ukamau group: 'Based on statistics we collected and taking into account the work of distributing our films among the peasants in the countryside, we calculate that in just one year approximately 340,000 workers, peasants and students came to see the films of our group' (1997:69).

Similarly, having completed *The Hour of the Furnaces*, the filmmakers began to explore 'parallel distribution circuits' for the film through trade unions and community organisations (Getino, 1997:103). The problem for Third Cinema, however, is that while monopoly capital tries to bury radical cinema by ignoring it, the state may take an unwelcome interest in an oppositional cinema. The direct or indirect influence of the state on film industries is common across the world. Even Hollywood has need of the American state in order to campaign or apply pressure on its behalf in foreign markets. And in those markets, already overwhelmingly dominated by Hollywood, the role of the state in encouraging and protecting indigenous industries through a variety of mechanisms (taxes, alternative public revenues, prizes, festivals, quotas and so on) is often crucial in sustaining national cinemas around the world (Johnson, 1993:204–8). For Third Cinema, however, the role of the state must be viewed as a problematic necessity. Of course the political coloration of the state does make a difference. For example, after 1973, with the ascension to power of a new democratic government in Argentina, Getino and others on the Peronist left joined the dominant film industry. Getino was appointed head of the film classification board which he made more progressive by opening the board up to a wider range of interest groups and ensuring that only pornographic films were cut or banned (Getino, 1997:106). Getino was criticised by some on the left who continued to argue for the necessity of the very film practice Getino had helped pioneer: a guerrilla cinema. Getino rightly argued that the new government had a massive popular mandate compared to the illegitimacy of the previous military rulers. Yet at the same time, Getino's rejection of a more militant cinema is symptomatic of an over-identification with bourgeois political rule rather than the *social* revolution which *The Battle of Chile* charts, despite the fact that here too was a progressive government with a large popular mandate. Argentina of course was to go the way of Chile with the return of the generals. Third Cinema must align itself with the Marxist ambition of extending the political revolution into the wider social body, which ultimately means the state must wither (Mèszàros, 1995:464).

A textbook case of the complex and indeed paradoxical relations between the state and the cinema can be found in the example of the Mexican film *Herod's Law* (Luis Estrada, 1999). Mexico has been ruled for more than seven decades by the Institutional Revolutionary Party (PRI). The Mexican state conforms very well to Octavio Paz's description of the typical Latin American state as a 'philanthropic ogre' (Johnson, 1993:204). With support comes bullying and intimidation and self-censorship. *Herod's Law* is a tale of political corruption set in the 1940s but with obvious contemporary parallels. It explicitly names and implicates the PRI in this corruption, which includes political assassination. (The ex-President Salinas de Gortari is currently a fugitive and is widely believed to have been involved in assassinations while his brother is in jail for laundering drug money) (Cox, 2000:5). The film had received government funding through the National Culture and Arts Council but the script which the Council had approved was changed during shooting to include the PRI by name. Moreover, while the original script had a conventional happy ending where the bad guys get punished, in the finished film the corruption pays off (Moore, 1999).

Once in the hands of the state film distributor (IMCINE), *Herod's Law* was subjected to a variety of dirty tricks, including a restricted release, cancelled screenings, even out-of-focus screenings. A popular outcry against these attempts to sabotage the film's access to the public resulted in IMCINE handing the film over to its director for his tiny company to distribute himself: a move designed to consign the film to oblivion. Except that a mysterious benefactor stepped in and offered the director finance for 250 prints to open the film nationwide. *Herod's Law* was subsequently a critical and popular success. There was speculation however that the mysterious benefactor was the right-wing opposition party PAN, whose party presidential candidate was the former head of Coca-Cola in Mexico. If true, then a leftist film has been used to undermine support for the right-wing PRI in the hope that another right-wing party, PAN, benefits in the elections (Cox, 2000:5). And in fact PAN did win the presidential elections in July 2000.

Squeezed between monopoly capital on the one hand and the state on the other, Third Cinema clearly exists within a very small space of opportunity. Despite this, Third Cinema has developed working practices inscribed with the values of co-operation, democracy, accountability and use-value, which are the negation of a system based on competition, hierarchical structural control over labour, élite control impervious to accountability and, above all, exchange value (Burton, 1997). It exists at all because of the contradictions within the system and the social unrest which those contradictions generate. The dominant First Cinema often acknowledges and taps into these contradictions and popular anxieties about and even resistance to the rule of capital. Yet, as we have seen, there are serious and profound limitations to First Cinema's representations, fully embedded as it is within the social relations of capital. In this chapter we have explored the Third Cinema critique of First Cinema and touched on some of the alternatives it offers. In the next chapter we explore the relations and differences which Second Cinema has to First and Third Cinema.

4 Dialectics of Second Cinema: The Bandit

This chapter explores the specificities of Second Cinema in relation to First and Third Cinema. Implicit in this will be the argument that Second Cinema represents in some ways an 'advance' on First Cinema but that it also falls short of the lucid social analysis achieved by Third Cinema. I am focusing this discussion through the figure of the bandit in Second Cinema. This will help us explore the dialectics between the three cinemas because the celluloid bandit has 'cousins' (such as the gangster) and manifestations in First Cinema and may be seen as anticipating the revolt of the masses in Third Cinema, a revolt that necessarily consigns the figure of the bandit – the individual, lone outsider – to the dustbin of history. After defining and giving a general survey of the celluloid bandit, I go on to explore three cinematic representations of the bandit in more detail: *Eskiya* (Yavuz Turgul, 1997), *Bandit Queen* (Shekhar Kapur, 1994) and *The General* (John Boorman, 1998).

HISTORICAL BANDITS AND CELLULOID BANDITS

Since celluloid bandits are often based on real historical figures (as is the case with *Bandit Queen* and *The General*) it is important that film criticism try to formulate an adequate understanding of the relationship between the historical roots of the phenomenon of banditry and their re-presentation in film. E. J. Hobsbawm's book *Bandits* (1969) is useful in this regard. Although a historian, Hobsbawm is as interested in the folkloric representation of the bandit in songs and stories as he is in more conventional sources of historical evidence. These songs celebrate what Hobsbawm calls the 'social bandit.' They 'are considered by their people as heroes, as champions, avengers, fighters for justice, perhaps even leaders of liberation, and in any case as men to be admired, helped and supported' (1969:13).

Even more significantly, while historically the bandit derives from peasant societies, the attraction of the bandit has always 'been far wider than its native environment' (1969:112). From oral story-telling to literature and then on into the twentieth century's industrial cultural forms such as film and television the bandit has an enduring fascination. This is not just a question of nostalgia. More significantly, the bandit is a repository of utopian hopes: 'the dream of justice' (1969:113). Thus the archaic becomes a vehicle for hopes of a different kind of future. Referring to Robin Hood, Hobsbawm notes that: '[w]hat survives from the medieval greenwood to appear on the television screen is the fellowship of free and equal men, the invulnerability to authority and the championship of the weak, oppressed and cheated' (1969:113).

Celluloid bandits, then, have a peculiar relationship to real history just as the earliest songs celebrating bandits did. Film criticism should not approach the cinematic representation of the bandit (even when based on real-life figures) and judge it against whatever historical evidence may exist. For the fact of the representation is itself evidence of a more profound historical reality: the social inequality which the bandit rebels against. Thus the meaning of the celluloid bandit is dependent on the historical *situation* that gave rise to real bandits and which continues to give rise to their representational forms. Judgement on the celluloid bandit must hold on to the significance of this situation and not become obsessed with the representation's accuracy to the deeds and misdeeds, the *empirical details* of the bandit's life.

THE BANDIT AND THE GANGSTER

The celluloid bandit must be distinguished from the figure of the gangster or bank robber. The gangster is, in Fanon's terms, an assimilationist, seeking access to capitalist wealth and imitating, even if in grotesque parody, bourgeois values. There is a long line of such figures in First Cinema, from *Public Enemy* (William Wellman, 1931) to *Scarface* (Brian de Palma, 1983).

By contrast the bandit is a figure who does not seek integration into the social order but operates on its margins, questioning its basic assumptions. The bandit does not seek wealth but revenge, justice or simply survival. In contrast to the figure of the gangster, the bandit retains some sort of connection with a *constituency of the oppressed*. The gangster, by contrast, represents a political blockage, their greed, selfishness and acceptance of the basic capitalist values of 'dog eat dog' competition fatally undermines any solidarity with the oppressed, even when, as is often the case, they come from a poor, marginalised background.

The gangster's inability to articulate a politicised relation to popular struggle is the explicit theme of the South African film *Mapantsula* (Oliver Scmitz, 1988). The film was made in the last years of the apartheid regime. Like Luis Estrada in making *Herod's Law*, the filmmakers circumvented the regime's apparatus of censorship by concealing the nature of the film being made. The South African authorities believed that the film was a conventional gangster film whereas *Mapantsula* (meaning 'spiv') explores the forces and charts the process (the very thing that *The Battle of Algiers* elided) which drives a small-time criminal to become politicised.

The narrative structure of the film is devised to underscore this process of change. It is split into two strands which unfold chronologically. One strand begins with the gangster, nicknamed Panic, arriving in the police cells which are full of township militants, to whom Panic is initially hostile. In the other narrative strand we see the events which lead up to Panic's arrest. These include a growing protest movement against rent increases, his girlfriend getting sacked from her job as a domestic help and a young activist whom he knows being murdered by the police. These experiences do not in themselves lead to his politicisation (as a linear narrative structure would require) for he arrives in the cells still seeing himself as a loner and tough guy. But the flashback structure allows these experiences to now be gradually reflected upon as he is beaten and bullied by the police who want him to sign a false confession that would implicate Duma, an activist. In the final scenes Panic is shown video footage of the clash between police and protesters. Panic is there on the tape, partly out of a growing concern and awareness of what is happening, partly out of coincidence. But now, as he watches himself and the protesters and as he has the confession in front of him, he joins the struggle and in answer to the demands that he sign, he utters an emphatic 'no'.

The celluloid gangster then may be viewed as a depoliticised response to social inequality. The gangster is the imagistic equivalent of that terrifying phrase 'If you can't beat them, join them.' This distinction between the bandit and the gangster does seem to have some historical veracity insofar as the latter has rarely been involved on the side of the revolutionary masses. By contrast, 'social banditry has an affinity for revolution, being a phenomenon of social protest'

(Hobsbawm, 1969:84). The nineteenth-century Cuban bandit Manuel Garcia supported the independence leader José Marti; Pancho Villa joined the Mexican revolution and Mao's Red Army was largely composed of former bandits (Hobsbawm, 1969:89–91). Thus in *Godfather II* (Francis Ford Coppola, 1974), when Michael Corleone attempts to extend his mafia business interests into Cuba on the cusp of the 1959 revolution, he recognises how formidable the revolutionary forces are but feels no affinity or identification with their cause.

If *Mapantsula* traces the movement from selfish spiv to politicised consciousness, the British heist movie *Face* (Antonio Bird, 1997) has the reverse trajectory as its premise. Ray, once a socialist and activist, has withdrawn from political struggle after more than a decade of defeats for the left in the UK. Now a bank robber, he discovers that even the paradoxical code of loyalty within the criminal fraternity has been eroded by the greed of the Thatcher/Major years. Meeting his mother, who is still involved in political struggle, he admits that while he does not give to the poor, he does steal from the rich. She is scathing and identifies his activities as the mirror-image of capitalism – a theme central to any good gangster movie. At one level, *Face* operates a Third Cinema decoding of the gangster film, firstly by grounding a primarily American genre in a specifically British context and secondly by making explicit the anti-capitalist critique which remains implicit within most gangster films. For although the gangster as a figure aspires to assimilate to the social order governed by Mammon, the narration of their trajectory (the comparison between capitalist business and the gangster's business) opens up a potential space for criticism of that order.

THE BANDIT AND FIRST CINEMA

The bandit does have a First Cinema incarnation, most popularly as the outlaw in the western genre. The link between the western outlaw and social banditry is implicitly acknowledged in *O Cangaceiro* (1969), a Spanish/Italian co-production which relocates the genre of the spaghetti western in Brazil. The same year saw Glauber Rocha's rather more well known *Antonio das Mortes*. This too is set in the *sertão* of north-east Brazil which historically was the home of the *cangaceiros*, Brazil's famous bandits. *Antonio das Mortes* has a 'spaghetti western' feel to what was anyway a highly stylised

inflection of the genre. The storyline traces Antonio's transformation from an agent of the military regime which has hired him to
hunt down bandits to a rebel himself. A similar contest between
outlaw and agent of the law is central to Sam Peckinpah's *Pat Garrett
and Billy the Kid* (1973). The hero of the film is the younger Billy,
who has chosen the more authentic life of the outlaw (having for a
time been on the other side of the law) whereas Garrett has chosen
to be the instrument of the law. The problem that the film has with
Garrett's choice and which the character of Garrett knows (and
regrets) only too well is that the law represents the interests of the
big landowners like Chisum and the railway companies. The bandit
is a romantic figure because the 'law' they abide by is generated from
within rather than enforced from without by socially compromised
agents. In *Pat Garrett and Billy the Kid* it is clear that Billy has the
sympathy and support of ordinary people, both whites and
Mexicans. But unlike *Antonio das Mortes*, the links between the
bandit and ordinary folk appear vaguely defined; that the bandit is
linked to a constituency of the oppressed is very muted, as it is in
various re-presentations of the Robin Hood legend, not least because
Robin Hood himself comes from the dominant feudal class which
he never really leaves.

THE BANDIT AND SECOND CINEMA

It is this link with a constituency of the oppressed that Second
Cinema affirms. In this way the bandit is perfectly suited to engaging
with the national realities ignored by First Cinema, whether that
First Cinema is the global product of Hollywood or the local/national
version. The bandit is necessarily an archaic figure, out of joint with
'modernisation' which often erodes what was good about 'past'
social relationships (for example, autonomous local communities)
and leaves intact what was bad and oppressive (such as poverty and
patriarchal structures). Historically, banditry:

> seems to occur in all types of human society which lie between
> the evolutionary phase of tribal and kinship organisation, and
> modern capitalist and industrial society, but including the phases
> of disintegrating kinship society and the transition to agrarian
> capitalism. (Hobsbawm, 1969:14)

While the emergence of capitalism intensifies exploitation and increases social stratification, thus opening up a new era of banditry, once 'economic development, efficient communications and public administration' have been established, the conditions for banditry diminish (Hobsbawm, 1969:15). This archaic quality of the bandit *vis-à-vis* modernisation recalls Fanon's discussion of the recovery of cultural traditions as a necessary but incomplete moment in the anti-colonial struggle. The bandit is an important repository of utopian revolt but ultimately the bandit's archaic quality consigns them to First and Second Cinema. The bandit cannot stay a bandit and attain what Fanon called 'the fighting stage', where modern political ideals of mass emancipation are conjoined with *reworked* cultural traditions. In the case of the bandit the reworking has to be radical; it has to be a dialectical transformation from individual or small group rebellion and social outsider(s) to collective politicisation and struggle.

From this point of view, it is clear that the bandit is an *ur*-figure (a primitive archetype) anticipating and evolving into the guerilla fighter or terrorist. In the 1970s in particular, left-wing groups such as the Red Brigades in Italy, the Baader-Meinhof gang in Germany and the Weathermen in the United States conducted themselves as urban bandits: secret organisations, on the run from the forces of the law, but in a mass urban society, with little or no relationship to the exploited classes they claimed to represent. Chabrol's film *Nada* (1974), about a group of left-wing terrorists (Nada, named after Spanish anarchists) who kidnap the American ambassador from a high-class brothel, is probably one of the best cinematic depictions of this impasse in political struggle. While the film reveals the ideological confusions and hopeless gulf between the group's means and ends, the state is revealed to be even more ruthless than the members of Nada. As the *Time Out* review put it with surprising clarity: 'it is the members of Nada, groping desperately to build little burrows of viable living in a world of expediency and corruption, who become the heroes in spite of everything' (1998:593).

If one evolution of the bandit forks into the politics of the isolated group (or even individual) operating within mass society, there is another evolution. Just as the bandit traditionally adopted villages in which each would protect the other, so oppressed constituencies such as the Palestinians, the Catholic minority in Northern Ireland and Mexican peasants in Chiapas have entered into similarly symbiotic relations with armed groups (the PLO, the IRA, the Zapatistas). These are defensive responses which represent the weakness and isolation of the oppressed constituencies in the face of powerful state organisations. They represent in real history the political blockage which the celluloid bandit in Second Cinema is symptomatic of: the tragic absence of a revolutionary alternative.

ESKIYA

Eskiya, meaning 'bandit', is the title of Yavuz Turgul's celebrated 1997 Turkish film (although it was co-financed by French and Bulgarian money, so that it was always intended for the international arthouse circuit). The story focuses on Baran who has been released after 35 years in jail. Arrested by the gendarmes in the Cudi mountains with his fellow bandits, the toll of the prison years has claimed the lives of all the bandits except him. What has kept Baran alive is love for a woman who, before he was arrested, apparently spurned him. First Cinema will of course use love as a theme but by making love and unrequited desire the primary means by which Baran has kept going, love, in a typically Second Cinema move, is elevated to a metaphysical level.

Baran returns to the mountains and his village home. He finds half the village deserted and in ruins and the rest of it submerged under water. An old woman, inhabiting the ruins like a ghost and the only remaining person, tells Baran that everyone was told to leave when the dam was built. As in *The Emerald Forest* the dam represents regressive modernisation: change imposed from the top down, with little or no consultation and resulting in the displacement of rural people into the overcrowded and poverty-stricken cities, is a familiar tale across the Third World. The old woman tells Baran that after he went to prison, evil triumphed and the weak were trampled upon. There is no doubt that the bandit as a figure who retains a strong link with the constituency of the oppressed is a romantic figure. This romanticism has the advantage of allowing the figure of the bandit to act as a rebuke to capitalist modernisation. What is lost within such romanticism is the particularity of banditry, its social and economic roots, and how the brutal conditions that give rise to the bandit in turn brutalise *him*. This romanticism does indeed appear to be gendered. It is striking, for example, that *Bandit Queen* eschews all such romanticism. Thus the outsider, a-social nature of the bandit must also be understood as articulating male fantasies of autonomy from the social order. The amulet that the old woman gives to Baran to protect him from the bullets of others is an indication of this fantasy to transcend the social order in which one is embedded – and transcend, of course, is very different from transform, which would be the objective of Third Cinema.

Baran moves on to find Mustafa, the man who told the police where to find him. If love is one theme that the film raises to a metaphysical level, then with the introduction of Mustafa two other themes are now deployed: waiting and betrayal. We find that Mustafa has been waiting for Baran all these years. Riddled with guilt, Baran's appearance is something of a relief, for now, in the sentence of death which he fully expects Baran to hand down to him, he can at least explain if not expiate his sins. Through Mustafa, Baran learns that his real nemesis is his former best friend, Berfo, who was behind Mustapha's actions. Berfo, it appears, wanted Baran out of the way so that he could steal his love, Keje. Berfo used money stolen by the bandits as his dowry and a reluctant Keje was forced by her father into Berfo's embrace. Having learned from Mustapha that Berfo and Keje are in Istanbul, Baran takes his leave. The theme of waiting is reproduced in the characters of Berfo and Keje and it is worth just considering for a moment why this theme is particularly suitable for Second Cinema. The idea of waiting as a condition of life would be an affront to First Cinema. Its linearity, its commitment to narrative, its embeddedness in the modernist principle of advancement, means that waiting as a pervasive suspension of life, is structurally precluded from it. Waiting suggests an essential emptiness to life, a suspension of action which has any meaning or substance on the part of those who wait. Again, such themes are too metaphysical for First Cinema, too intangible.

Baran travels to Istanbul which only serves to further underline the distinction between the archaic and the modern. Here Baran struggles to cross roads and to understand how television works. On his way to Istanbul he makes friends with a young petty criminal, Cumali. He is acting as a drugs mule for a local mid-level crime boss, Demircan. When the police are waiting for him at the train station, Cumali swaps his bag with Baran and begs him to take it to Demircan's garage and headquarters. This Baran does and, anticipating later events, barely in time to rescue Cumali from a beating, or worse. In return, Cumali pays for his room in a crumbling hotel and Baran is drawn into Cumali's poverty-stricken neighbourhood.

Baran shares the hotel with a motley collection of other oldsters washed up on the shore of an uncaring and brutal society. There is the aging whore who gets beaten up by her pimp; Andrei Mishkin, a bitter Russian émigré who hates capitalism and communism in equal measure; and there is Kemal, an old actor too ill to find regular work. Later he will hang himself. The film makes a self-reflexive lament on behalf of cultural workers through Mishkin, who sees the way society treats its artists as an indicator of its wider condition. Cumali meanwhile notes that his father named him after one of Yilmaz Güney's screen characters. Güney, a popular actor and director, was imprisoned in 1972 for sheltering political militants and again in 1974 for shooting dead a right-wing judge. Güney famously made two films by proxy from prison, *The Herd* (1978) and *Yol* (1982); the latter was completed in exile.

These self-conscious, intertextual references to culture are characteristic of Second Cinema. First Cinema, by contrast, is extremely wary of addressing the issue of culture at all, except in terms of biopics where the artist's individuality can be foregrounded. However, *Eskiya*'s comments on the marginality and ill-treatment of the artist in Turkey are also typically (for Second Cinema) abstracted from any concrete specificity concerning their social location. The artist is just another group sucked into the despairing condition of modern life.

The theme of betrayal is woven around the character of Cumali in particular. He is in love with Emel whose brother is in prison. The brother in turn is desperate to escape but needs money to bribe officials to get a transfer to the low-security medical centre. Cumali promises him that he will raise the money. In order to do that, Cumali and his gang strike a deal with the vicious Demircan. But the grinning faces and nervous laughter of Cumali's gang show just how out of their depth they are. At one level Demircan is 'betrayed' by Cumali, who steals some drugs to finance Emel's brother's escape. Except that her brother turns out to be her lover and, once free from prison, Emel runs off with him. Enraged, Cumali searches the city and, finding them in a hotel room, he shoots them both, thus repeating a family tragedy. Cumali's father was cuckolded by his stepmother and he too shot them both.

The cyclical and pervasive quality of betrayal in the film raises it, like love and waiting, to a metaphysical level. It becomes part of the human condition; a generality beyond social and historical determinations, it is simply woven into the affairs of men and women as a given. Baran and Berfo, Cumali and Emel: this heavy patterning of betrayal into which all the characters are inexorably drawn gives betrayal the quality of fate.

Second Cinema then, like First Cinema, resists social and historical specificity. Despite the emotional and psychological complexity it achieves over First Cinema, despite the fact that Second Cinema differentiates itself from First Cinema by searching out those areas of life that First Cinema represses, Second Cinema transforms its particular stories into stories of the human condition every bit as mythic as First Cinema. While First Cinema is generally quite positive and affirmative of the capacity of *individuals* to change their circumstances, Second Cinema tends to be more pessimistic, hence the importance of cyclical structures and motifs, repetition or the prevalence of psychological breakdown (Bordwell, 1979).

Running parallel to Cumali's story is of course Baran's. He searches the streets of Istanbul for Berfo and Keje. At the level of the street, the city reminds him of prison; but when he gets onto the roof of the hotel and he looks out across the top of Istanbul, it takes on the quality of the mountains he knew 35 years ago. It is on the hotel roof that Cumali bleeds to death (thus making him an honorary bandit) after he has been shot by Demircan's thugs on the streets and it is on the rooftops of the city that the bandit too will meet his fate. His search on foot however proves fruitless. He finds Berfo instead via the television when he appears on a news item. Berfo, now under another name, has become a hugely wealthy and powerful man. The news item reports on questions concerning the fine line between Berfo's legal and illegal financial activities.

Although Demircan tells Baran that now all the bandits are in the city, the film itself distinguishes between the bandit and the 'gangsters' that inhabit the city. At the bottom of the pile there are the petty thieves such as Cumali and his gang and the pimps; at the mid-level there is Demircan's organised crime and at the top there is Berfo, where legal and illegal capital fuse. However, Berfo's criminal activities are only hinted at in the news report and the film itself does not explore Berfo's business activities any further. Perhaps this is because, more than any other area of criminal activity in the film, the fine lines between big business, the law and illegality would draw attention to the social and historical specificity of capitalism. By alluding to but not exploring Berfo's business dealings, Berfo takes up his place in a world where everyone is on the make to some extent: once again, a particular component of life is elevated to a general human condition which bypasses the social and historical determinations on that condition.

Baran finds an unrepentant Berfo wheelchair-bound and suffering from emphysema. Keje meanwhile has not spoken for 35 years. Discussing Güney's film *The Herd*, Krespin draws our attention to the culturally specific image Keje can be located in:

> The characterisation of Berivan in *The Herd* strongly relies upon a recurrent motif in Turkish folk culture, in which the image of a beloved woman is frequently used as a metaphor for God, a prophet or the Motherland. Frequently silence or muteness symbolises the fact that the woman is hurt because of the suffering inflicted upon her by the insensitive or the unjust. The folk poet who deeply shares the suffering of his wounded beloved usually begs her attention and forgiveness by asking her to talk to him, even if it is only a single word. (Krespin, 1983:5)

Similarly, Keje's muteness symbolises the suffering of the nation which is evident in the streets of Istanbul. More immediately, it is Berfo who is the source of her wounds and sorrow. Yet it is Berfo who has spent the years begging her to talk to him. Berfo declares his love for Keje but he measures his love in acts of betrayal which make it impossible for Keje to reciprocate. When Baran appears before her the first thing she asks is whether it is still true that bandits turn into stars when they die. This anticipates Baran's coming death but also weaves another metaphysical discourse around the figure of the bandit, further disembedding him from social and historical particularity.

When Cumali is captured by Demircan and threatened with death for stealing a cut of his drugs, Baran goes to Keje to ask for help. Together, they go to Berfo's headquarters, the bandit looking hugely incongruous in the context of a hi-tech corporate building. Berfo gives Baran a cheque and in return Keje has promised to stay with Berfo. The cheque however bounces: once again Berfo has betrayed Baran, this time because he could not comprehend how Keje's life could be equal in worth to Cumali's. As a result, Cumali dies. Baran avenges him, killing Berfo and then brazenly walking into Demircan's garage, shooting half-a-dozen of his men before ascending to the office where he finds and executes a trembling Demircan. Back in his hotel, the pimp who has been beating up his whore bumps into Baran who casually shoots him as well just for good measure. There is something of a First Cinema resolution here and indeed the tough guy who avenges the weak is a popular figure within mainstream Turkish cinema.

The final scenes however return to the metaphysical register of Second Cinema. On the rooftops of Istanbul the bandit's luck runs out. He loses his magic amulet after a brief skirmish with the police. As he walks towards the edge of the roof while the police fire volley after volley, fireworks explode in the evening sky. Over the edge he goes but he fades away into the night. Keje, looking out her window, sees a star flash across the sky and then the film cuts to the old woman on the Cudi mountains and she too, looking up at a glowing star, bids the bandit goodbye. This immortalisation of the bandit may also been seen as tapping into the folkloric need for bandits to avoid death. This, Hobsbawm suggests, 'expresses the wish that the people's champion cannot be defeated' (1969:43).

BANDIT QUEEN

Bandit Queen (Shekhar Kapur, 1994), which was co-produced by the UK television company Channel Four, had an impact in western film markets that few Indian films have achieved. The positive reception of the film in the west was determined by three factors that were likely also to have been calculated by Channel Four: *Bandit Queen* had journalistic value, it was aesthetically congruent with western notions of 'realism' and the centrality of gender and the oppression of women had a resonance with western audiences which other areas of Indian life might not have had.

The journalistic value of the film lay in the fact that the story, written by Mala Sen, was closely based on the life of Phoolan Devi, who became India's most famous bandit in the early 1980s. Her release from jail at the same time as the completion of the film fortuitously continued the tie-in between real bandit and celluloid bandit, while subsequent events, such as the banning of the film in India, Devi's initial hostility towards the film (she was later reconciled to it) and Devi's continued troubles with the authorities, all gave the subject (and therefore the film) a high profile in the media.

The second reason for the film's success in western markets is much more crucial from a Third Cinema perspective. Aesthetically, *Bandit Queen* sits very comfortably in a tradition of Second Cinema realism. It is a tougher, more explicit realism than *Eskiya*, which, as we have seen, incorporates many metaphysical elements. *Bandit Queen* is solidly 'realist' in terms of performance style, use of locations, lighting, editing, overall temporal structure and, above all, the graphic depiction of violence and sexual abuse. Indeed it was this last characteristic which made the real Phoolan Devi recoil from the film when she saw the violations and humiliations heaped on her screen self represented so explicitly (Sen, 1994). Certainly within India the film did break new ground in terms of explicitness but violence and sex (and their interrelations) have historically been the taboos that Second Cinema has confronted and, in so doing, generated controversy (Birri, 1997a:88). From a Third Cinema perspective, the question and value of explicitness should not be conflated with the question and value of a social and historical analysis.

From a western perspective, *Bandit Queen* was judged to be a breakthrough in realism when judged against the dominant Bombay-based film industry within India, sometimes known as 'Bollywood'. As one American film critic put it: 'In India, where a large movie industry produces a stream of silly musicals, mediocre soap operas and raucous action flicks, a film like "The [sic] Bandit Queen", with its gorgeous photography, strong production values and urgent social criticism, is rare' (Guthmann, 1995).

This cheerful ignorance, which assumes that alternative film traditions do not exist in India, is coupled with terms of praise that uncannily match the aesthetic preferences found in 'progressive' First Cinema. How surprised this critic would be to find a filmmaker like Kumar Shahani questioning some of the basic principles of First Cinema, from Hollywood to Bollywood:

> The traditional mechanistic structure with the beginning, middle and end is a dramatic structure which originated in the nineteenth century in Europe. It was closely related to the methodology of physical science – cause and effect in a chain. As far as I know, science today goes beyond this and accommodates fluctuations. One has to find new ways that are linked to actual perceptions. Ritwikda and Kosambi made me probe into the epic form. You also see it all around. It enters the consciousness of people in such a way that they can take it home with them. (Baghdadi and Rao, 1995:109)

The epic form's first major theorist and practitioner was of course Brecht, who devised a form based around a looser structural and temporal organisation that resembled montage more than linear causality. Another filmmaker working in the epic form is Ketan Mehta, whose 1981 *Bhavni Bhavai* draws on the Indian performance style of Bhavai (a synthesis of acrobatics, drama and music), comics and cartoons, and the colours of Gujarat folk paintings to offer a critique of the caste system. Mehta's later film *Mirch Masala* (1986) also deploys similar folkloric traditions, allegory and a magic realism closer to Latin American cinema than western cinema (Baghdadi and Rao, 1995:29–40). Like *Bandit Queen*, *Mirch Masala* is a critique of patriarchal gender relations but in a style that is unlikely to be viewed very favourably by western film critics imbued with the naturalistic traditions of realism. As we have seen in relation to Pontecorvo's two films *The Battle of Algiers* and *Burn*, western film criticism is very much more ready to valorise certain formal strategies over others, which is fine, except it is done with little critical reflection on the assumptions which underpin such aesthetic preferences.

The third factor that facilitated *Bandit Queen*'s positive reception in the west was the centrality of gender in the film. An Indian film focusing on Indian politics, for example, or the tensions between modernity and tradition, might have struggled to reach sufficient audiences. While *Bandit Queen* is not exclusively concerned with gender (it also engages with the question of caste oppression) the film's most powerful imagery figures brutal male authority oppressing women. This obviously keyed into the recent history of gender struggle in the west. Evident in some examples of the critical reception of the film was a sense of superiority concerning western progress on the issue. 'Ironically, it may inspire Western moviegoers to think more highly of our own society's record on women's rights, despite whatever inequities remain. Considering the alternative portrayed here, maybe we're not doing as badly as we thought' (Rosenberg, 1995).

These three factors, the journalistic, the aesthetic and the familiarity of the gender issue, help explain why this film received financial backing from Channel Four and why that backing was repaid by the film's critical success in western markets. This is not a final judgement on *Bandit Queen* but it does start to relativise some of the very favourable responses which the film achieved.

Certainly *Bandit Queen* is a savage indictment of Indian patriarchy, the servile role it imprisons women in and its close intertwining with the caste system. This 3000-year-old social hierarchy condemns those at the bottom to a life of poverty, humiliation and suffering. The élite castes view the poor as physically and spiritually unclean, hence their term for them: the untouchables. The growing political strength, organisation and confidence of the untouchables is evident in their own preferred (and rather more accurate) term for their social location: *dalits*, a Hindi word meaning 'the oppressed' (Burke, 1999:37–43). Thus to be a women and a *dalit* is to be as far down the social ladder as it is possible to go.

A quotation from Hindu religious scriptures opens the film and gives a sense of the values of the caste system and the valueless life to which those at the wrong end of it are consigned: 'Animals, drums, illiterates, low castes and women are worthy of being beaten.' This quote is juxtaposed with a non-diegetic frontal shot (reminiscent in some ways with the non-diegetic closing shot of the outlaw in the early cinema classic *The Great Train Robbery* (1903)) of the lead character who declares to camera: 'I am Phoolan Devi, you sister fuckers.' On the one hand then we have the full weight of tradition embedded into Indian society over many centuries, and on the other the film asserts a strong individual who resists meekly succumbing to this tradition. The film foregrounds Phoolan Devi the rebel who from the time she was a child had a fiercely independent streak. Thus the film's contextual powers are rather diminished by this emphasis on the individual.

So too is any sense of the historical origins of Phoolan's defiance. There are hints in the film that she is close to her mother but we never find out anything about her mother who may well have passed down to her daughter the seeds of rebellion that were sown in earlier times. Her mother must have matured in the late 1930s and '40s. These were tumultuous times for India: what movements, politics and changes touched her life? We never know and so one possible explanation, one avenue of historical contextualisation, is shut down to us.

Nevertheless, the film offers a devastating portrayal of Indian men. The first half of the film consists of a cycle of rapes. In the pre-credit sequence we see Phoolan being sold to her husband Puttilal for a cow and a rusting bike. She is eleven years old. He rapes her. Puttilal's mother hears her screams and quietly withdraws from the house. The complicity of other women in the oppression of women is another theme in the film. Phoolan returns to her parents. After the credits Phoolan, now a young women, is set upon by Ashok whose father is the headman of the village which is run by the high-caste Thakurs. Unsurprisingly, the village elders condemn the victim and order her to leave the village. She goes to stay with her cousin

Kailash. Kailash has links with local bandits to whom he delivers supplies. Here the film misses an opportunity to explore the symbiotic relations between villagers and bandits. Why Kailash has these relations is never explained. The film appears to suffer from not utilising a voice-over narration, despite the fact that it is based on the dictated prison diaries of the real Phoolan Devi. The issue of Kailash and the bandits, as with Phoolan's mother, could have been introduced via a voice-over. However, a partial linkage of the film's narration to the subjectivity of the central protagonist appears to be ruled out by the film's commitment to that mode of 'objective' realism which we have encountered in relation to *The Battle of Algiers* and Italian neorealism.

Kailash functions simply in plot terms to provide a link between Phoolan and the bandits. Kailash's wife however is jealous of Phoolan and forces her to leave. Returning to her village she is arrested by the police ostensibly to question her about the bandits. However, they also rape and beat her. Her bail is paid by Thakurs connected to the headman of the village. It is clear that further sexual violence awaits her were she to go with them so she returns to her home. The Thakurs however pay bandits led by Babu Gujjar to kidnap her. He too rapes her repeatedly. The cycle of rape culminates in her being gang-raped in 1980 at Behmai village over three days. The routine manner in which these rapes are carried out and the lack of any effective legal safeguards implies that such sexual violence is deeply entrenched, widespread and common. However, apart from one scene which we will come to later, the film's central focus on Phoolan Devi means that we only ever see this social and sexual power being directed at her. There is a sense then that these sexual assaults are responses to Phoolan's personal militancy; punishments directed against her to crush her individual spirit. Contrast this with the following news report about an incident in 1996:

Bhuli Devi, a 30-year-old peasant woman, stands naked in a field on the edge of her tiny village in Samastipur district, in the central northern state of Bihar. She has been accused of stealing four potatoes from a landowner's field and so has been stripped and forced to stand at the scene of her alleged crime for several hours. It is very hot. Her accusers, and her judge and jury, stand around laughing at her. They are led by the farmer on whom her family's livelihood depends. When it gets dark they will gang-rape and kill her. (Burke, 1999:38)

When Phoolan is judged by the village leaders after Ashok has
tried to rape her, both she and her poor family have to bow and
scrape before the public power of the Thakur caste. Yet despite the
visibility of caste differences, the socioeconomic relations, the interconnections between caste and property, property and power, which
are so evident in the above report, remain invisible in the film. One
could look at the village and simply see people divided by caste but
essentially homogeneous in terms of property relations.

While the film separates the question of caste from its socioeconomic dynamics, it is better at exploring the relations between caste
and gender, particularly once Phoolan Devi joins the bandits. When
she and Kailash meet the bandits, a mutual attraction is sparked
between Devi and one of them, Vikram Mullah, who is also a lower
caste. Because of this he is not the leader of the gang. When the
bandits kidnap Devi under the orders of the Thakurs, it is being led
by Babu Gujjar. His repeated raping of Phoolan causes Vikram to
spark a lower-caste mutiny when he kills Babu. Vikram's own
position at the bottom of the caste system clearly facilitates an identification with Phoolan's plight. 'We should respect women,' he tells
his men.

Indian bandit mythology has it that there is no caste system
within the bandit kingdom. But there clearly is. Vikram's gang is
visited by a senior bandit leader who warns that he sees hatred of
Thakurs in Vikram's eyes. He is also concerned that Vikram has
integrated a women into the gang. But Phoolan and Vikram become
lovers. Their first time together and Phoolan's first consensual sexual
experience is a rather fraught, tense, rough affair (she slaps him, for
example), marked as she has been by all the previous violations.
Having established a genuinely caste-less bandit gang, the film
further demonstrates the close link between banditry and the constituency of the oppressed when the gang 'adopt' a village. In return
for distributing stolen money to the poor and making an offering to
the gods, the village swears to protect the bandits.

However, this revolt of the oppressed within the bandit kingdom
is fragile and weak. The true leader of the gang is the Thakur bandit
leader Sri Lam. When he and his brother, Lala Ram, are released from
jail the police chief discusses the scandal that a low caste and a
woman are now in charge. The scene establishes the close common
(caste) interest which the law and the outlaw can have in crushing
this new and threatening development. Hobsbawm has noted that
historically the bandit's social situation may be an ambiguous one.

The bandit must often seek alliances or working relationships with local powers. The more successful they are as bandits, the more they are liable to develop mutually beneficial interlocking relations with other powerful groups and organisations (Hobsbawm, 1969:79–81).

To return to *Bandit Queen*, this mutuality between Sri Lam and the police chief is underlined by the scene's cinematic strategies. The camera begins behind Sri Lam and Lala Ram as they are sitting down discussing the situation with the police chief. The camera tracks back as Sri Lam tells the police chief that he will reassert control over his gang. The camera spins round 180 degrees and the *mise-en-scène* shifts to the corridor outside the room. At the end of the corridor some police men are casually beating up a women. The film then cuts back to a frontal shot of the bandits assuring the police chief that he can control Vikram, while the beating continues to take place, slightly out of focus in the background. In this way the caste rebellion of Vikram, the gender issue and the shared interests which the police chief and Sri Lam have in reasserting 'normality' are brilliantly conveyed. This is the only time we see another woman on the receiving end of male brutality.

Sri Lam's return to the gang causes immediate tensions. Then Vikram is shot while bathing in the river. Sri Lam is obviously behind the assassination attempt but Phoolan is more concerned to get Vikram to a city doctor. There we find them holed up in their room. The location of the city brings with it a number of signifiers of modernity. They have sex wearing sunglasses with Phoolan on top. Even more daring, Vikram asks to see her completely naked; 'That's how they do it in the city,' he tells her. This traditional taboo on the naked body – even between lovers – prepares the (western) audience for appreciating the horror of Phoolan's ultimate humiliation. Leaving the city they return to Phoolan's parents. Her father still wants her to return to her husband, Puttilal. Angered by this, Phoolan agrees but she has something other than reconciliation in mind. She metes out a savage beating to her estranged husband with a rifle butt.

However, another attempt, this time successful, is made on Vikram's life by Sri Lam. Once again Phoolan is beaten up and finds herself surrounded by men with guns and power over her. Sri Lam takes Phoolan to Behmai village where she is gang-raped in a barn over the course of three days. Sri Lam then strips Phoolan naked and in front of the village parades her degraded and beaten body, mocking this so called 'Queen of the Ravines'. To complete the humiliation and her forceful return to the submissive role assigned to women, he orders her to draw water from the village well. Sri Lam's only mistake (from his point of view) is that he does not kill Phoolan.

Having recovered from her ordeal, Phoolan, helped by Kailash, meets up with a former comrade of Vikram, Man Singh. Together they go to see the regional bandit leader who assents to Man Sing and Phoolan setting up another gang. This is a political decision since the bandit leader notes how much support Phoolan has amongst the low-castes. 'What can a woman do?' he asks his adviser.

Phoolan's response is to commit an audacious raid on a large town. Here we glimpse some sense of class as a socioeconomic relationship. The shopkeepers are desperately trying to hide their goods and close their shops while the bandits tell the poor that they have nothing to fear. Then, learning that Sri Lam is attending a wedding at Behmai village, Phoolan leads the gang to avenge herself. However, Sri Lam cannot be found and the village men who are assembled in the courtyard, in front of the well where Phoolan had to draw water, will not give him up. The tension mounts as does Phoolan's anger until, spontaneously, her men begin shooting. The historical record shows that 22 men were killed that day. For the first time (in at least a long time) upper-caste Thakurs were on the receiving end of avenging violence on a large scale. The massacre at the village brings a massive and brutal response by the police. Gradually her gang are gunned down. Two years after the massacre, Phoolan surrenders to the authorities. The surrender is a ceremonial event. A large crowd chant, 'long live Phoolan Devi' from behind the police lines. The film's writer Mala Sen notes how, 'Thousands gathered to watch...having walked several miles through the dusty pathways that crisscross the Chambal Valley – the badlands of central India – in order to catch a glimpse of a living legend' (1994:6).

Yet the film itself does not really do justice to the connection between Phoolan and this constituency of the oppressed. So relentlessly does the film focalise everything through Phoolan (there are only three scenes – two of them very brief – which she is not in) that the viewer does not get a sense of how she is viewed by the poor. We see them chanting her name, but from a distance. How much more effective it would have been for the spectator to have 'entered' the scene in the company of some of those people who walked the dusty pathways across the Chambal Valley to see their heroine. Such a focalisation would have brought out the politics of their identification with her. Philip French has argued that: 'Sen and Kapur use Phoolan's career to anatomise a whole society, the way Francesco Rosi did with the life of a comparable Sicilian social bandit in the Marxist classic *Salvatore Giuliano* (1961)' (1995:9).

On the contrary, as we have seen, the film plays down almost as far as it is possible to do so the socioeconomic dimensions of caste divisions and plays up the individual dimensions of Phoolan Devi's admittedly extraordinary but still socially explicable story.

THE GENERAL

John Boorman's *The General* (1998) might seem a peculiar film to discuss in terms of the celluloid bandit. The film is set in Dublin in the 1980s and early 1990s rather than the rural and mountainous terrain of *Bandit Queen*. *Eskiya* may be largely set in Istanbul, but Baran comes from traditional bandit country. Furthermore, *The General* is based on the real-life figure of burglar and crime boss Martin Cahill. Taking their cue from this real historical reference point, critics categorised *The General* as a gangster film. My contention however is that the celluloid Cahill is a bandit not a gangster. It is the historical situation of the bandit rather than the dynamics of the gangster that structures *The General*. It is this profound historical reality that the film is true to and against which the film should be understood. Some critics worried at the absence of certain empirical details which would have revealed the real Cahill to be more prone to violence than the celluloid Cahill (Mullin, 1998:6). This misses the point however. The film transposes the historical situation of the bandit to Cahill in order to convey a set of class dynamics. The question that occurs concerns how this transposition comes about. There are three key factors involved: Boorman's authorial 'code'; the significance of the film being shot in black and white, and the way the real location of Dublin and Ireland saturates the film.

We have seen that the bandit is something of an archaic figure and so would be a natural magnet for a director with Boorman's interests in the pre-modern (*The Emerald Forest*) and the mythic (for example, the 1981 film *Excalibur*). *Point Blank* (1967), Boorman's first feature film, is a hard-boiled gangster/thriller that weaves an unexpected dialectic between the cutting edge of modernity and that which has been left behind. Lee Marvin plays Walker who is double-crossed and left for dead in the abandoned jails of Alcatraz during a money-laundering operation. After the pre-credit sequence in which we see the double-cross that leaves Walker seemingly fatally wounded, we see Walker on a tourist boat circumnavigating the infamous island prison. Over the loudspeaker we hear the tour guide tell us that no escapee ever made it across the treacherous waters. How then did Walker do so, after being shot several times? The answer, of course, is that he did not. Walker is a ghost (although the film never actually shifts into the supernatural) who returns to haunt the crime syndicate with his remorseless request: 'I want my money.' Because we are invited to read Walker at one level as a ghost, it is no surprise that he can drift through the Organisation's security systems. This ghostly quality underlines what an archaic, out-of-date figure he is in a world where the Organisation has become like any other big business, with its hierarchy of smartly dressed executives. He cannot comprehend why these executives do not carry large quantities of money around with them. The transformation of the money economy by capitalist modernisation (banks, money transfers, cheques, credit cards) has left him behind. As we shall see, in *The General* Cahill has a similarly archaic relationship to money.

The second factor determining the mapping of the bandit onto the figure of Cahill is Boorman's decision to shoot the film in black-and-white. One critic remarked that this gives an 'attractive texture' to the film that sentimentalised the story (Williams, 1998:8). It is true that there is some romanticisation of character in this film but, as we have seen in *Eskiya*, this is hardly unusual at least in the case of the male bandit. However, the romanticisation is moderate and is only a major problem if one sees the film as a passive reflection of a real life. There is however a more important effect resulting from the use of black-and-white film. Discussing his decision, Boorman writes:

> In *The General* there were many street scenes where I could not control the colour, streets drenched in the lurid poly-plastic colours of the contemporary world: acid-yellow anoraks, brick-red Toyotas, electric-blue neon lights. In black-and-white, film approaches the condition of dream, of memory, reaches out into the audience's unconscious. There was often a mythic dimension to black-and-white movies. They presented a familiar yet alien world, a contiguous reality. (Boorman, 1998:4)

In *Point Blank* the archaic figure of Walker works because at one level, as I have suggested, he is a ghost from the past. In *The General*, however, the film has to wrap an older world around Cahill. To do this it must push 1980s/90s Dublin back into the past by screening off, or at least dampening down, the visibility and presence of the object world of contemporary capitalism with its 'lurid' colours incessantly demanding our attention. The reference to black-and-white movies is suggestive of how the film works to drive its material back in time, an exertion which constructs a parallel 'contiguous reality' rather than a passive document of a life or period.

It would be easy but mistaken to graft Fredric Jameson's argument about postmodern nostalgia on to *The General*. For Jameson such nostalgia is the retro-chic of a society whose only relationship to history resides in a celebrated 'inauthenticity as the sign of a now socially marginalised Real...in a spurious image culture' (1992:218). On the contrary, Boorman's strategies are devised precisely to give some articulation to a repressed history. Boorman's authorial code and the decision to shoot in black-and-white is working to (re)construct the archaic within the modern, to construct, that is, the historical conditions in which the bandit can emerge. The final piece in the jigsaw of this process comes from the location itself: Dublin and Ireland. For while the country is part of western Europe, it shares with parts of southern Europe a relative backwardness, the persistence of the social influence of Catholicism which has played a role in retarding capitalist modernisation, a weak or fractured national territory and, until very recently, a predominantly rural economy. This relative backwardness creates the conditions in which the bandit can flourish. On the one hand there are riches to be robbed but on the other the police force is patently too provincial, amateurish and low-tech to combat Cahill's cunning. Thus it is that the film is able to recreate, within an urban setting at the tail-end of the twentieth century, the historical situation of the bandit.

The General begins with Martin Cahill's death. It is August 1994. A crane shot over the suburban rooftops of Dublin drops down into one of the streets, with their picket fences and neat gardens, to find the unassuming Cahill coming out of his house. He is dressed in jeans and a leather jacket. He gets into his modest Renault 5 but as he starts the car an assassin races out from behind a bush and shoots him dead. Cut to the police station where it is announced to cheers that 'Tango One is down'. Back at the scene of the murder, the press are gathering and questioning Inspector Kenny on accusations that the police were in a tacit alliance with the IRA who have declared responsibility. As in *Bandit Queen*, the authentic bandit is an enemy to those on both sides of the law. By beginning at the end the film will unfold with the foregrounded aim of accounting for this antagonism towards the police and a paramilitary organisation. It also requires the film to use the flashback structure which helps drag the events further back into the past in order to recreate the archaic territory of the bandit.

We flashback to Cahill as a boy, hurtling with an armful of stolen booty down the narrow alleyways of the Dublin slums and across the estates where he lives. He is being pursued by the Garda but as they enter his territory (the estate) they are set upon by the residents who spontaneously impede their way with missiles. This first flashback is essential for establishing Cahill's class roots which provided him with his sense of identity and indeed the entire purpose of his antagonism towards the police authorities. The Hollyfield estate, which comes to the young Cahill's aid, provides that special bond with place and people that is typical of the figure of the bandit. Later in the film Cahill and his gang will carry out an audacious raid on a jewellery firm kitted out in soccer team jogging gear with the name Hollyfield United emblazoned on the back.

Despite this life-long identification with Hollyfield, the estate itself is physically destroyed and the residents re-accommodated in new housing. Cahill arrives back from a spell in prison to find the bulldozers moving in. Although now married to his boyhood love, Frances, and despite having kids, Cahill refuses to move out of his flat. This exertion of power by the local authorities is too much for him. Cut to a caravan surrounded by the debris of the bulldozed estates. Interestingly, an Irish flag flutters ironically in the breeze. Cahill emerges to find the caravan surrounded by police, a priest and local authority figures. They try to 'reason' with him, but he has nothing but contempt for them: 'Fuck off the lot of you – cos you're all oppressors of the poor; civil fuckin' servants...parish fuckin' priests – get the fuck out of me house.'

This defence of the estate, of his own kind, of the place that has sustained and protected him, is just like the bandit and the mutually beneficial relationship they establish with the village. In the next scene Cahill returns home one evening to find his caravan burning. Cut to the next scene and Cahill is emerging from a tent he has set up next to the burnt-out shell of the caravan. The plans of the authorities, with their destruction of communities in the name of top-down progress and unaccountable change with little meaningful consultation, are similar in structure to the dam as emblem of regressive modernisation which we have already come across in *The Emerald Forest* and *Eskiya*. Cahill's action, while limited by its individual and largely symbolic nature, is entirely understandable and not at all irrational.

The film moves on to charting Cahill's increasingly successful career as a burglar. We see him creeping around a large house, miner's lamp illuminating the way, helping himself to the contents of the fridge (food is always a vital part of the tribute paid to the bandit). He sees a husband creep out of his wife's bed and enter the waiting au pair's room. This reference to the hypocrisy of bourgeois marriage anticipates later events when Cahill's personal relations take an unexpected and unconventional turn. Cahill and Frances's sister Tina fall in love and even have children. But Cahill does not leave Frances, nor is he having an affair. Everything is open, acknowledged and honest between the three of them. They happen to love one man. He happens to love two women. This affront to bourgeois culture is just one of the many things that make Cahill inexplicable to the police. Staking out his house towards the end of the film, one of them will ask, 'Which sister did you screw last night? Both?' To which Cahill replies, 'Yours.'

It is however Cahill's large-scale robberies involving his gang that earn him the sobriquet of 'the General'. Bandits are often given such nicknames. The great Brazilian *cangaceiro* Virgulino Ferreira da Silva was known as Lampiao (the Captain). The first bank robbery we see comes as a result of Frances's persuading Cahill to buy the house in suburbia. This offends his class sensibilities. 'You'll be playing golf next,' he says. But she reassures him: 'It's still us against them.' Nevertheless, this modest spending of his illegally acquired wealth makes him uneasy. He is emphatically not like the assimilationist gangster. He does not spend his money in consumer sprees (later he will say that 'You don't own things, they own you') nor does he invest the money in other markets as corporate capitalism would. Instead, he stashes his money in the Irish countryside. In this archaic attitude to money, Cahill is strikingly similar to Walker in *Point Blank*. However, while Frances has found a house, the buyer will not take cash. So Cahill enters the bank and unloads £80,000 in exchange for a banker's draft. He then gets his men to rob the bank while he goes to the police station to talk to Inspector Kenny to cement the perfect alibi. When one of the officers breaks the news that the bank has been robbed he remarks to Kenny that it is a 'disgrace the profits these banks are making'.

It is this class perspective which the film repeatedly articulates that makes it closer to an example of Third Cinema than either *Bandit Queen* or *Eskiya*. Casing the Alfred Beit collection of paintings, Cahill explains the source of this immense wealth when Frances asks how anyone could get this rich. Beit owns a diamond mine in South Africa, where 'blackies' dig out the precious stones and are X-rayed to make sure they do not swallow any. Legal capitalist business makes Cahill's own activities look small fry in terms of the money stolen and positively benign against capitalist exploitation. By comparison, Cahill always insists that the money stolen by his gang is divided up into equal shares.

Cahill's success however brings him into conflict with the IRA who want half of the money from the audacious raid on the O'Connor job, which the IRA had cased but then rejected as too difficult. Cahill refuses to be bullied. Later, Sinn Féin-run community groups mobilise the people against Cahill to counter his popularity. We have already seen local people queuing up in Cahill's pool room to help themselves to free essentials. 'It's my way of paying taxes,' he explains to one of his men.

After the Beit job, the police intensify their round-the-clock surveillance on Cahill and his men (although, mysteriously, the police disappear on the morning of Cahill's assassination). Here their provincial pettiness comes through as they throw stones at him and release a stoat into his garden to kill his beloved homing pigeons. The simplicity with which he outwits their low-tech operation is wonderfully comic. Needing to get to the stolen paintings but followed constantly by the police, he simply gets in a car and drives around the countryside for several hours. When the car runs out of petrol he takes out a spare canister and fills up. The police have no such reserves however and when they run out of petrol Cahill simply carries on driving.

The other major organisation with which Cahill has to negotiate is the Ulster Volunteer Force to whom he sells an Old Master painting. When they meet, the UVF proclaim their loyalty to the Queen. Again, Cahill's response brings out the class relations in such an identification. Expressing his ironic admiration for the Queen he notes that 'her ancestors murdered and tortured and grabbed every bleeding thing they could. And she doesn't pay taxes. She's my hero.'

Cahill then, like the bandit, is an outsider, a rebel. He is antagonistic to all forms of institutional authority, to the police, to the world of commerce and consumerism, to bourgeois values, to nationalism and loyalism. The only positive relation he has to group identity is the strong class identification to his past on the Hollyfield estate. But increasingly, as his old friends from the estate are picked off by the police, it is an imaginary bond with little actual legitimacy. Thus *The General* is best viewed as allegory (that is to say, it tells a bigger historical story through a particular story) and in particular as an allegorical lament on the *absence* of a class-based alternative to the bourgeois politics of national identity (Loyalism and Republicanism) which has dominated Ireland's troubled relations with its Imperial neighbour.

This chapter has explored the cultural and symbolic resonance of the bandit, contrasting him/her with the figure of the gangster on the one hand and mass struggle on the other. I have suggested that the representation of the bandit does have some relationship to history but it is less the empirical details of the lives lived by individual bandits that matter. The history that the bandit speaks to is more structural and epochal, a history of class societies, of combined and uneven development, of the historic tensions between the country and the city, of exploitation and oppression. It is for these reasons that a theory of Third Cinema must be interested in the figure of the bandit. Within the Second Cinema incarnations of the bandit that I have looked at in this chapter, the archaic bandit prefigures the future collective resistance to the social inequalities which Third Cinema makes it its task to discover and equip people with the cognitive and emotional resources to change.

5   Dialectics of Third Cinema

In exploring the dialectics of Third Cinema, this chapter seeks to construct a dialectical relationship between the now and the original historical moment of Third Cinema's emergence between the mid-1960s and mid-1970s. This requires a focus on Latin America as the theoretical and political crucible of Third Cinema. I am seeking to construct a dialectical relationship both in terms of Third Cinema film practices, then and now, and Third Cinema theory, then and now. A dialectical relationship between then and now recognises, at both the level of film practices and film theory, the threads of continuity that connect us with the past as well as the transformations in theory and practice provoked by new historical contexts. This dynamic accounts for the films discussed in this chapter which in one way or another demonstrate transformations and continuities in the strategies and concerns of Third Cinema. I explore the shifts to allegory and satire in *The Voyage* (Fernando Solanas, 1990) and *Miss Amerigua* (Louis R. Vera, 1994) and generic transformations of the musical in *Evita* (Alan Parker, 1996) and *Dollar Mambo* (Paul Leduc, 1993).

In exploring the original historical moment and theoretical orientation of Third Cinema, I will focus on Solanas and Getino's seminal essay 'Towards A Third Cinema'. I also want to explore a work that functions as a bridge between this original moment and more contemporary theoretical and practical concerns; I am referring here to Cuban filmmaker Tomás Gutiérrez Alea's 1980s essay 'The Viewer's Dialectic'. This essay represents a major theoretical statement by a working filmmaker and is at least as important as anything written by Eisenstein and Brecht (both important influences on Alea). However, it has received comparatively little attention, another sign perhaps of the 'Eurocentrism' that dominates cultural criticism. I finish the chapter by drawing together the main themes and issues of Third Cinema via an analysis of *The Elephant and the Bicycle* (Juan Carlos Tabío) which was, appropriately enough, Cuba's contribution to celebrating the 1995 centenary of cinema.

A PHILOSOPHY OF MEMORY

Against this dialectical relationship with the past, many contemporary political and theoretical positions advocate a kind of forgetting and so we must offer as a counter-strategy the importance of memory. One of the central assumptions of modernism as a social, political and economic force is that we can and must leave the past behind, look to the future and put our trust in progress to resolve the conflicts and problems that have dogged our ancestors. In his social history of the nineteenth century, mediated through a study of Paris, Walter Benjamin found this blind belief in progress – in the inevitability that things will get better, that social problems would be resolved by industrial, technological and scientific developments – to be an article of faith. The world fairs in which the latest commodities, innovations and marvels of the age were exhibited were the 'holy shrines' to this secular religion called progress (Buck-Morss, 1989:87–95).

Crucially, this attitude, in which eyes are turned forever towards the future, views the past as having nothing to offer the present, as having no resources to provide, no lessons to offer. From a Marxist perspective, this attitude is profoundly problematic. First, it tries to persuade the latest generation to forget about the injustices and betrayals of the past. As Benjamin noted:

> Social Democracy thought fit to assign to the working class the role of the redeemer of future generations, in this way cutting the sinews of its greatest strength. This training made the working class forget both its hatred and its spirit of sacrifice, for both are nourished by the image of enslaved ancestors rather than that of liberated grandchildren. (Benjamin, 1999a:252)

Second and perhaps more importantly, the belief in the inevitability of progress is demonstrably naïve. Industrial, technological and scientific developments will never deliver their utopian promises as long as they are enmeshed in the social relations of capital, with its dynamics of profit accumulation a priority and the interests of the vast majority of the human race negligible.

Third, it is clear that social, political and economic modernisation is actually secretly wedded to something very traditional, well established and (from a Marxist point of view) out of date: the

maintenance of capital in perpetuity. In this crucial respect, modernisation is not about change at all.

In contrast to this forward-looking, blind faith in progress and
apologia to private property, Benjamin formulated a different
philosophy of history, famously using a painting by Paul Klee to give
metaphorical expression to this philosophy. In Klee's 1920 painting
of an angel (*Angelus Novus*) Benjamin finds the 'angel of history':

> His face is turned toward the past. Where we perceive a chain of
> events, he sees one single catastrophe which keeps piling wreckage
> upon wreckage and hurls it in front of his feet. The angel would
> like to stay, awaken the dead, and make whole what has been
> smashed. But a storm is blowing from Paradise; it has got caught
> in his wings with such violence that the angel can no longer close
> them. This storm irresistibly propels him into the future to which
> his back is turned, while the pile of debris before him grows
> skyward. This storm is what we call progress. (Benjamin,
> 1999a:249)

The angel of history moves into the future with his back to it, not
knowing what it will bring. But he can have no illusions about the
future for he sees clearly enough, as he is propelled into it by the
storm called 'progress', the destruction, waste and death upon which
the present is always built.

Benjamin wrote these lines in 1939 on the eve of the Second
World War, when the rise of fascism cast a huge shadow across
Europe. If the circumstances made Benjamin understandably over-
pessimistic concerning the possibility of progress (the angel 'sees one
single catastrophe'), it is a philosophy of history that is still relevant
to our times. For Argentina the hopes for political and social change
that inspired 'Towards a Third Cinema' ended in the mid-1970s
when Isabel Perón's right-wing and increasingly authoritarian
regime was overthrown in a military coup with clear fascist
intentions. Between 1975 and 1981 between 10,000 and 30,000
people 'disappeared'. In Argentina these years are known as the
'Dirty War' in which the state tortured and killed leftists of all per-
suasions. The question today for Argentinians is whether to forget
the past and 'move on' or remember the past and demand justice
for wrongs that were done. For the Mothers of the Plaza de Mayo,
who have gathered in front of the presidential palace every Tuesday
for more than 20 years, there can be no forgetting of lost loved ones.

The dead must be redeemed and, if only symbolically, made whole by recognition, remembrance and repentance. Meanwhile, the political and economic élites in contemporary, bourgeois democratic Argentina have another agenda, as this newspaper report suggests: 'President Carlos Menem, who was himself imprisoned for five years, has made it clear that he finds the examination of the past a distraction from the task of reforming the economy and making Argentina an investment paradise' (Scott, 95:9).

The Chilean writer Ariel Dorfman has noted that it is not only the generals and entrepreneurs who want to forget, but that memory can be painful to those who suffered directly or indirectly from violence (Dorfman, 1997:21). Patricio Guzman's significantly titled documentary *Chile: The Obstinate Memory* shows the divisions still bubbling away under the surface of national progress and unity, post-Pinochet. Interestingly, Guzman uses his own earlier film, *The Battle of Chile*, to provoke a debate about what is remembered and how it is remembered. Having screened the film to young teenagers, we watch a debate unfold between those who say Pinochet was necessary and those who ask what kind of progress it is that is built on tyranny and murder. A screening to older students of *The Battle of Chile*, students who would have been young children during the coup, provokes a different response. Here we see not disagreement but the collective pain which results from being emotionally and psychologically part of this history and the realisation of the tragedy they and their parents have been repressing.

The pain of memory is also the theme of *Black Flowers* (Lita Stantic, 1992), a Channel Four, Argentine and Mexican co-production. As with many co-productions, the story involves travel, where an outsider enters a different society and culture and struggles to understand it. In *Black Flowers* Kate Benson (Vanessa Redgrave), a British filmmaker, arrives in Argentina to shoot a script written by Bruno, an old Argentine leftist. The film (within the film) is set during the Dirty War and is based on the life of an estranged friend of Bruno's, Sylvia, whose lover, an activist, was kidnapped and killed by the security forces. Sylvia however, who learns about the film, has recently married and wants to forget about the past, but finds the film project stirring up painful memories. The film then is structured around two stories: Kate Benson's attempt to research the past in order to understand the context of her film, and Sylvia's attempt (unlike Benjamin's Angel) to fix her eyes resolutely on the future. However, at the end of the film, she takes her teenage daughter (with whom she was pregnant at the time of her lover's disappearance) to see one of the old abandoned buildings used by the military as a torture centre.

As Ariel Dorfman notes, something painful can be repressed but it always resurfaces in other ways. And this is as true for collective, public memory as it is for individuals. The past can never be left behind and repressing it tends to tie one to the past even more strongly and detrimentally than if the pain and violence suffered is acknowledged. Given that such ties often take the form of compulsive repetition, the worst-case scenario would be for history to repeat itself. Moreover, such public amnesia, Dorfman argues, is a way of shaping our identity in the present, an identity which Chileans and Argentinians are encouraged to think means absolute and unquestioning reconciliation with capitalism and the free market (1997:21). And not only them. A film like *Black Flowers*, with its co-production financing and address to different audiences (Latin-American and UK) suggests that we are indirectly connected by the historical fall-out of what happened in Chile and Argentina (Grant, 1997). After all, in the UK, There Is No Alternative (TINA) has been the mantra of Prime Ministers from Thatcher onwards, while Pinochet's coup in Chile was the laboratory for the American-inspired economic policies that Thatcherism subsequently implemented.

CULTURAL IMPERIALISM

If we are to rescue Third Cinema from internment in the past, then we must rescue it from the enormous condescension of the present. This requires a double critique. For the first wave of Third Cinema theory and practice was powerfully marked by the larger critical paradigms of dependency theory and notions around cultural imperialism that were dominant in the 1960s and 1970s. These paradigms attempted to explain the unequal political, social and economic dynamics that structure relations between the west and the rest, while cultural imperialism concerned itself specifically with the importance of culture within those relations of force. While illuminating in many instances, the cultural imperialism model has come to be seen as problematic for a number of reasons. Briefly, these are:

a) there is a tendency to read cultural effects straight off from political and economic relations;

b) the notion of 'core' nations (particularly the US) dominating 'peripheral' nations fails to subject the national question to any critique – specifically the privileging of 'national culture' does not address the way the national is fractured by other divisions, such as class, gender and region;

c) connected to this over-homogenised view of the national culture is a failure to think through a more complex model of trans-national cultural exchanges and influences, not all of which are baleful and many of which have become part of the national culture, while not all cultural exchanges are unidirectional, even if they are profoundly unequal;

d) the notion of cultural imperialism tends to impute a certain passivity and/or false consciousness to the consumers of western cultural products which is patronising, simplistic and fails to take into account the possibility of indigenising media products in ways which make them relevant to immediate, local circumstances;

e) the cultural imperialism model tends only to see inequalities between one sector (the west) and another (the rest) which represses unequal political, social and cultural relations *within* these sectors.

For example, it could be argued that the UK is substantially influenced by US cultural imperialism. There is a culture of deference to US foreign policy while UK economic policy is strongly influenced by US ideals as it is in other areas, such as employment and law and order. And of course 'culture' in the more specific sense is very evident in Hollywood's domination of UK film screens. The cultural imperialism model would be tempted to read off the latter example against the political and economic examples. It would suggest that Hollywood films help cement consent to the pursuit of US political and economic models so favoured by UK élites. It is possible to think that there may be thematic links between the tough image which agents of law and order have in Hollywood films and increasingly authoritarian policies in this area. But it is quite another thing to suggest that there are *causal* links where one functions to reinforce the implementation and acceptance of the other. Moreover, such an interpretation tends to fail to do justice to the films themselves, which are often a good deal more complex and ambivalent than they initially appear, and this opens up the possibility for readings by audiences that do not simply and unequivocally support the agents of law and order.

I suggested that a double critique has to be made because it is not only the critical paradigms within which Third Cinema initially emerged that need to be examined and problematised. Although the complications and unevenness of the world picture often proved too much for the cultural imperialism model, it still had the great merit of identifying political, social and economic inequalities and suggesting, sometimes oversimplistically, that there is a *link* between these *material* realities and the cultural flows and exchanges, the diversity (or otherwise) and repertoire of meanings and identities which culture provides. And this attempt to forge a *link* is preferable, I would argue, to the newer more fashionable paradigms in which such material inequalities virtually disappear in favour of a world picture of multiple dynamics and flows too complex and too unpredictable to shape into any kind of structured pattern. The key paradigm that has displaced the older paradigm of cultural imperialism is postcolonial theory. Although space does not permit a substantial engagement with postcolonial theory, I do want to give some flavour of its themes and its problems by focusing on an essay by the influential postcolonial literary critic Homi K. Bhabha.

POSTCOLONIAL THEORY: MEANS AND ENDS

According to Bhabha: 'Postcolonial criticism bears witness to the unequal and uneven forces of cultural representation involved in the contest for political and social authority within the modern world order' (1999:190).

This is an admirable ambition and very much within the tradition of the cultural imperialism model. The problem however is that the methodologies which postcolonial criticism are wedded to are largely in conflict with this ambition. There are elements within the postcolonial critique that are valuable (although not necessarily unique to it). The critique of the 'claims to the continuity of an authentic 'past' (Bhabha, 1999:190–1) which is so central to national identity, has been well made, although Marx made the same point over a hundred years ago in *The Eighteenth Brumaire of Louis Bonaparte*. The emphasis on transnational cultural flows linked to migration and displacement also helps to problematise the national model of cultural imperialism. Bhabha's notion of 'translation' has been very influential in foregrounding the active processes by which cultural material is transformed across time and space. However, these gains are bought at a tremendous political and explanatory loss.

Postcolonial theory has been influenced by poststructuralism (a linguistic theory which argues that meaning is generated by difference) and postmodernism (which argues that culture, with all its plastic, malleable and shifting qualities, is the all-powerful and embracing force and model of the (post)modern era). Both influences are highly relativistic, providing little foundation on which to organise a politics of progressive change, and both are profoundly idealist in the philosophical sense that it is ideas, values, beliefs, or (to use the preferred term) *discourses* that constitute the ultimate horizon of explanation.

For Bhabha, the main project is to explore the transnational as the space of translation, which is to set a decidedly cultural focus and agenda in its marginalisation of the social, economic and political forces which structure that space unequally. This culturalist focus cannot be easily reorientated since it is generated logically from the methodology. Following poststructuralism, postcolonialism argues that meaning is generated by difference, hence the importance of the *other* or alterity within the theory. Crucially though, meaning is not just generated by the difference between *x* and *y* (hence bringing some definition to each), but difference is also *inside* the subject or object which is perpetually on the cusp of becoming different from what it is at any one moment in time and space. This introduces a radical contingency to meanings, values, beliefs, the result of which is a profound 'indeterminism in cultural and political judgment' (Bhabha, 1999:192). Bhabha quotes Hortense Spillars as an example of how 'difference' has permeated historiography: 'the cultural synthesis we call "slavery" was never homogeneous in its practices and conceptions, nor unitary in the faces it yielded' (1999:196).

Let us use this 'insight' to re-write the end of Alea's film *The Last Supper*, which I discussed in Chapter Three. There we found the slaves revolting against their exploitation on a Cuban sugar plantation. Now we can imagine the priest rushing to intervene, carrying his well-thumbed essays by Bhabha and Spillars and declaring that their iniquitous treatment is only one 'face' of slavery or, better still, using his fingers to sign in quotation marks 'slavery'. Their revolt, the priest would point out, is premised on imposing a mythic unity (hence the quotation marks) on the seething diversity and differences that constitute life. The priest would argue that their conditions of life represent only one instance in a multiple array of discontinuous possibilities that might constitute 'slavery'.

Bhabha writes that 'contesting subjectivities...are empowered in the act of erasing the politics of binary opposition' (1999:196), but it is not clear what grounds there can be for contestation when everything is governed by difference. (Marx, by the way, was deconstructing binary oppositions long ago, but using dialectics, rather than difference as his key methodological principle). Where can the lines of solidarity and opposition be drawn long enough and hard enough within this methodology? Bhabha formulates his sense of how postcolonialism mobilises a political position in the following passage:

> It singularizes the 'totality' of authority by suggesting that agency requires a grounding, but it does not require a totalization of those grounds; it requires movement and manoeuvre, but it does not require a temporality of continuity or accumulation; it requires direction and contingent closure but no teleology and holism. (Bhabha, 1999:201)

Here we see all the pressures, contortions or sheer blandness erupting in Bhabha's discourse as he tries to give some grounding to a position based on discontinuity and contingency. Bhabha is trying to mobilise the authority required in a *particular* instance, to give individual and collective agents some grounds for action. However, one could accuse the theory of rank opportunism if that authority for action did not have some *continuity* with other instances, so the 'singularity' so prized here may not necessarily be the highest ethical principle. One can see ranks of politicians who state one policy or position in opposition, only to adopt another policy or position once in power, looking very relieved at the notion of 'singularity'. 'How could you,' they would say, 'compare what I said then with now. They are unique singular moments.'

Bhabha then goes on to argue that the grounds on which one builds a position on any singular issue or any singular moment should not be totalised. Once again, the opportunist, pragmatist and careerist breathe a sigh of relief. But there is something paradoxical about this position as far as postmodernist principles go. Postmodernism likes to think of itself as hostile to anything remotely 'absolutist' in thought, and yet what could be more absolutist than the proposition that all of life is to be understood as having the indeterministic properties of culture? Finally, Bhabha calls for 'contingent closure', which is rather like admitting that you have not discovered all there is to know about something for all time. Hardly very radical. Nor is there anything very unique in rejecting teleology, while rejecting 'holism' smacks of a rather holistic closure on everything from alternative medicine to green politics or Marxism.

The problem then with postcolonial theory is that it has an undialectical approach to difference and particularity. It collapses theory into difference and particularity, it fetishises them. As we have seen, the pursuit of difference is unable to sustain a politics concerned with radical change. It is also profoundly contradictory to its own one-sided principle, since the pursuit of difference can only be premised on a vulgar idealism that makes everything conform to the same basic principle and have the same basic characteristics of nebulousness. Politically, this results in a position remarkably similar, in the nervousness it displays to making overt and firm commitments, to the older liberal humanist cultural tradition. This older liberal humanist tradition (Culture with a capital 'c') is also highly undialectical, but in the other direction, towards universality. As Terry Eagleton notes:

> What Culture itself cherishes is not the particular but that very different animal, the individual. Indeed it sees a direct relation between the individual and the universal. It is in the uniqueness of a thing that the world spirit can be most intimately felt; but to disclose the essence of a thing means stripping away its accidental particulars. (Eagleton, 2000:55)

This was precisely what the bourgeois liberal critics found so pleasingly reassuring about *The Battle of Algiers*. What they perceived as the film's 'objectivity' is another way of saying that the film did not wallow in the particularity of the situation by taking sides: it transcended this to make a statement about the 'human condition', a concept which obviously does not want to get too bogged down in the nitty-gritty particularities of colonialism, exploitation, resistance, historical contexts, Islamic culture, and so on.

Dialectical thinking by contrast strives to undo these polarities. It strives to find the particular in the universal and the universal in the particular. An example of the former is implicit when I ask what the *particular* national-cinematic determinants were on Solanas and

Getino's Third Cinema manifesto. But I will still be looking to find the (historically determined) 'universal' lessons within their writing, by which I mean why it remains relevant to us today.

CONTEXTUALISING 'TOWARDS A THIRD CINEMA'

In order properly to appreciate Solanas and Getino's seminal essay 'Towards a Third Cinema', we have to situate it within the national context of Argentina and in particular the history of the film industry within that country. From the time of the first silent feature films, such as *Amalia* (Enrique García Velloso, 1914), based on a popular national literary classic, Argentina had a progressive First Cinema, rooted in national culture and including a strand of films which engaged in political and social criticism, such as *Juan sin ropa* (*Juan Without Clothes*) made in 1919 about the oppression of anarcho-syndicalist unions (Barnard, 1986:145–7). This progressive First Cinema culminated in a 'golden age' in the 1930s, before being displaced by a more bourgeois and Europeanised cinema as the industry became dominated by large capital and a new generation of filmmakers were drawn from the ranks of Argentina's expanding middle class (Barnard, 1986:44–5). This class shift and geo-cultural reorientation towards European classics resulted in Argentinian cinema losing audiences both nationally and across Latin America where it had for a while competed successfully with Hollywood.

In the mid-1940s, under Perón, the Argentinian state became increasingly involved in regulating and encouraging film production, which continued to be dominated by middle-class values and European sources. State involvement in the film industry intensified after a military coup in 1955 which ousted Perón. In 1957 the military government established a National Cinematographic Institute to encourage non-commercial cinema. While it was independent of commercial pressures, it was very dependent on state patronage. This Second Cinema returned to Argentine literary sources for inspiration but it was both élitist and politically quietest (Birri, 1997a; Dagron, 1986). In 1963 a new military government came to power and in the context of increasing opposition and resistance to the generals widespread censorship was implemented.

It is in a context then where neither First Cinema nor Second Cinema is able or willing to address the urgent social and political conflicts wracking the country that Solanas and Getino set up *Cine*

Liberacion in 1966, a guerrilla film group working in clandestine conditions. The group produced their ground-breaking, state-of-the-nation documentary *The Hour of the Furnaces* in 1968 and, in 1969, their equally ground-breaking theoretical reflections appeared in the journal *Tricontinental*, in which they coined the term 'Third Cinema'.

The essay 'Towards a Third Cinema' reflects the fact that an auteurist Second Cinema overly dependent on an authoritarian state had run into the sand while a progressive First Cinema had been extinguished several decades previously. These particular and immediate conditions within the national context impact detrimentally on the essay in the undialectical formulations of First, Second and Third Cinema. The first two are seen as dead or dying and having little or no resources to provide Third Cinema. Their model presents three discrete cinemas, with no interaction or reciprocal dynamics. While this is understandable given the particular circumstances of their time, it is a limitation if we are interested in continuing Third Cinema as a theory and practice outside of that particular temporal and geographical context.

ON THE ROLE OF THE INTELLECTUAL

One of the strengths of Solanas and Getino's seminal essay is the reflexiveness it demonstrates about the social location of the class to which the authors themselves belong: the intelligentsia. As Getino was to comment in a later essay, they understood themselves as 'middle-class intellectuals caught up in insurrectionary mobilizations, influence[d] by the cultural and political traditions of the working-class movement' (1997:102). Thus it was important to ask what the traditional role of the middle class had been within neo-colonialism, when direct external political and economic control had given way to more subtle networks of influence. The situation is still 'colonial' in the sense that there is an unequal concentration of power located elsewhere: in the headquarters of financial institutions like the World Bank, the IMF, the Wall Street stock market; in the boardrooms of the multinational companies operating within Latin America, and in the political capitals of the west, especially Washington.

Such international blocs of power influenced Argentine life via the national bourgeoisie who correctly perceived how their interests interlocked with those of international capital. Below the bourgeoisie, the actual owners of large capital, are the middle class, who:

were and are the best recipients of cultural neo-colonialism. Their ambivalent class condition, their buffer position between social polarities, and their broader possibilities of access to *civilization* offer imperialism a base of social support which has attained considerable importance in some Latin-American countries. (Solanas and Getino, 1997:38)

What Solanas and Getino refer to as imperialism is the manifest social and economic inequalities evident within Argentina, the under-utilised natural resources which it has at its disposal and the political authoritarianism required to contain the discontent which this situation generates. The middle-class domination of the media, education, politics, administration and cultural apparatuses plays a crucial role in normalising this situation, neutralising, absorbing, containing or eliminating any attempt at decolonisation: 'the fight for national independence' (Solanas and Getino, 1997:39).

For Solanas and Getino, the doctor, the scientist, the cultural worker, the teacher, even the priest, need not align themselves with the dominant political and economic groups nationally and internationally. They can instead choose to align themselves with the subordinate and exploited classes: the peasants and the workers. Indeed liberation theology is a classic example of the way religious ideas – exported to aid colonial control by persuading the poor and the oppressed that their time will come in Heaven – became indigenised and rooted in the life experiences of the poor in such a way as to be turned (by militant priests) against the existing social structures.

Increasingly then, a minority of the middle class were becoming radicalised in the post-Second World War period. In the mid-1950s, the Argentinian revolutionary Che Guevara – himself from a slightly impoverished respectable middle-class family – was travelling around Latin America. This journey opened his eyes to the awful hinterland of Latin-American life outside the sophisticated metropolitan enclaves like Buenos Aires. Still at this time studying medicine, Guevara was planning what he called 'a very pretentious book', entitled *The Role of the Doctor in Latin America*. Although the book was never finished, some chapter sketches remain. Essentially Guevara was mapping out the role of the revolutionary doctor. That role included acquainting themselves with the needs of the people, raising their class consciousness, stressing the importance of good health in daily life and, most importantly, aligning themselves against the authorities and with the people (Anderson, 1997:135–6). This sounds very similar to the role of the cultural worker as mapped out by Solanas and Getino. As Paul Willemen has noted, Third Cinema is not a cinema 'of' the people or simply 'for' the people. There are, inevitably, class relations that have to be negotiated. 'It is a cinema made by intellectuals who, for political and artistic reasons at one and the same time, assume their responsibilities as socialist intellectuals and seek to achieve through their work the production of social intelligibility' (Willemen, 1989:27).

Social intelligibility however is a process of 'discovery' (Solanas and Getino, 1997:47), as it was for Brecht and Benjamin; it cannot be a simple immersion into a populism (of First Cinema) which has too little confidence in the audience's ability to engage with complex modes of arrangement and expression (Solanas and Getino, 1997:47). Still less can it be a handing-down of truths from a position of superior (middle-class) knowledge. The intellectuals must be prepared to interrogate many of the assumptions and values that they have internalised from an early age. This includes the élitism of their cultural background (including its more benevolent paternalistic manifestations), their attachment to specialised discourses that shore up their own expertise, the separation of politics from art as well as from economics, their distance from popular struggles, their conformity, their attachment to material and cultural status at the expense of others, their attachment to competition and the refusal to make connections, treating each issue as discrete and thus avoiding the cumulative evidence that the current social order is unsupportable. Like Brecht and Benjamin, Solanas and Getino were attempting to persuade the progressive elements within the middle class to break with their class. However, as Benjamin noted, while you may leave your social class, your social class does not so easily leave you (Benjamin, 1982), hence the emphasis on a process of mutual learning. These issues are still crucially important to understanding the role of the intelligentsia (including academics) and the contours of contemporary cultural theory and practice around the world.

THE NATIONAL QUESTION

Solanas and Getino's essay is at one level a plea against simply and uncritically borrowing models – whether they are political, economic, cultural or aesthetic – from different geo-historical contexts. They are critiquing the slavish and unquestioning devotion to western metropolitan trends and to the mind-set of the Argentinian intelligentsia which sees Europe as the centre of civilisation, while Latin America is perceived to be 'so far away from things', as one Argentine writer interviewed in *The Hour of the Furnaces* puts it. The *uncritical* adoption, rather than the adoption *per se*, of European thought and models displays a contempt for the popular culture, experiences and impoverishment of the Argentinian masses. Moreover, Solanas and Getino argue that it imposes values which they see as prescriptive and irrelevant to the national conditions of Argentina.

> Our time is one of hypothesis rather than of thesis, a time of works in progress – unfinished, unordered, violent works made with the camera in one hand and a rock in the other. Such works cannot be assessed according to the traditional theoretical and critical canons. (Solanas and Getino, 1997:49)

This is strikingly undogmatic and open-ended and recalls Benjamin's advocacy of Brecht's cultural practice as a 'dramatic laboratory rather than a finished work of art' (1982:29). Yet while they never reject international cultural influences *per se*, the possibility of *productive* relations with western culture remains unacknowledged and untheorised. The conceptual blockage here revolves around the national question. The specific working-class tradition that Solanas and Getino were influenced by was a left-wing version of Peronism, which tried to bolt together the two great conflicting ideologies of the period of decolonisation: nationalism and socialism. 'In the neocolonial situation two concepts of culture, art, science, and cinema compete: *that of the rulers and that of the nation*' (1997:35).

The problem with the bourgeoisie and the middle class which coordinates its systems and structures is that they are not authentically of the nation. This not only lumps together all the various classes or class fractions who do not belong to the ruling class, it also implies that if the élites could become more orientated towards the life of the nation, addressing its needs, then the fact that they are élites would be less of a problem. This of course opens up the political space and strategy of left Peronism, although the contradictions between socialism and national reconstruction under enlightened political and economic élites were to unravel the Peronist project in the mid-1970s.

On the one hand then, Solanas and Getino's aspiration towards authentic nationhood, blocks analysis of the transnational cultural influences that may be influencing their own theory and practice. After all, the very concept of the nation and the divisions of Africa and Latin America into nation-states derives from European sources and domination over these terrains (Sreberny-Mohammadi, 1997:52–3). On the other hand, the impending realisation of authentic nationhood blocks analysis of the internal historical dynamics that *already* constitute the nation. This is a typical problem with the cultural imperialist model (Golding and Harris, 1997:5). As we have seen, the development of First and Second Cinema in Argentina was the result of a dual process that involved influence from foreign models *and* an 'internal' dynamic: the consolidation of the industry, the influx of second-generation middle-class filmmakers and the involvement of the state in fostering a national Second Cinema. And while Second Cinema may have run into an impasse within Argentina in the late 1960s, the institutional space for a Second Cinema culture (Argentinian and International) is clearly a prerequisite for the formal and experimental quality of *The Hour of the Furnaces*.

The nation-state is a real historical force. Over several centuries it became the dominant mode for shaping social, economic, political and cultural forces within a delimited territory on the one hand and intertwining that territory with the globalising dynamics of capital on the other. The nation is not then, as Bhabha suggests, merely a 'myth' (1999:191). Yet 'the nation' is not a category adequate to explain its own dynamics. The ideal of autonomy which is central to the concept (and which Third World anti-colonial forces invested massively in, for understandable historical reasons) cannot admit that in practice all nations are integrated into international dynamics. The extent to which élites do admit an international context of determinants on their actions calls into question the ideal of sovereignty (as the contemporary question of political and economic integration within Europe testifies). Even the US does not have autonomy from international affairs, hence its aggressive inter-ventionist foreign policy. The nation-state's assumption of sovereignty from a global context is matched by its reluctance to address internal differences (class, region, gender and so on).

Although *The Hour of the Furnaces* is rightly critical of the way the appeal to 'universal' values and culture disguises class specific values and culture, the film does not extend this critique to the concept of national culture and values.

Thus for Third Cinema, the national question is fraught with problems. It cannot be ignored since it is a real historical force, providing both a crucial context in which to make its interventions and one matrix of cultural resources with which to actually 'speak' those interventions (Willemen, 1989:20). On the other hand, its ideals do not match up to how nation-states actually operate and how they actually operate does not match up with that fundamental transformation in the mode of production that socialism and Third Cinema seek.

FICTION AND DOCUMENTARY

Solanas and Getino's critique of consumer capitalism is a familiar rendition from the critique of cultural imperialism (Tomlinson, 1991;122–39). It is one of the most problematic strands in their analysis. For Solanas and Getino 'films, the most valuable tool of communication of our times, were destined to satisfy only the ideological and economic interests of the owners of the film industry' (1997, 33).

Cultural theory has rightly moved on from such economic reductionism. The problem is that it does not allow for the particular qualities of cultural labour which may have some room for its own manoeuvre despite the elaborate apparatus of control and surveillance that capital puts into place. What is also missing from this reduction of film to the economic interests of capital is the question of the audience. They have to be engaged with, their passions, their fears, their anxieties, their hopes and aspirations, not all of which can be contained within or unproblematically met by a society dominated by capital. The crucial category missing from Solanas and Getino's essay is utopianism: the way popular culture draws on authentic feelings and desires for a life better than the here and now. Once we construct a model that allows First Cinema to be more contradictory than Solanas and Getino allow for here, then First Cinema also becomes a potential resource for Third Cinema.

Against the fantasy and fiction of dominant cinema, they pose the documentary film 'as perhaps the main basis of revolutionary filmmaking' (Solanas and Getino, 1997:46). This follows logically on from their problematic homogenisation of First Cinema (it was a position which both directors were to reassess fairly rapidly). However, the valorisation of documentary is also problematic in that it is potentially at odds with their broader critique of all the channels of cultural education (1997:38), which surely includes the dissemination of news and information. 'In a world where the unreal rules, artistic expression is shoved along channels of fantasy, fiction, language in code, sign language, and messages whispered between the lines' (1997:46). Yet that last section on coded and whispered messages seems equally if not more applicable to the daily news media, with their subterranean agendas or their highly selective, transient and neutralising adoption of popular concerns, where the questions they *don't* ask are more significant than the ones that they do ask.

We can perhaps say that Solanas and Getino's choice of the documentary film as the main cinematic strategy did make some sense given the particular historical conditions of the moment. As Alea notes, during periods of 'social convulsion, reality loses its everyday character...The dynamics of change, the trends of developments...are manifested more directly and clearly than in moments of relative calm' (Alea, 1997:129). In these situations, Alea argues, documentary, with its ability to engage with the urgency of the here and now, is the ideal strategy to pursue. This of course does not mean that documentary passively reflects the real world unfolding before the camera lens. It still requires an act of cultural labour, or what Birri called the poetics of the transformation of reality, to make that world intelligible. Recognising this, Solanas and Getino display a valuable non-prescriptive openness as to the forms, strategies and sub-genres to be deployed. '[I]t would be absurd to lay down a set of aesthetic work norms' (1997:47). Despite their problematic valorisation of documentary over fiction, their openness to diverse strategies within the documentary form begins to deconstruct the fiction/documentary binary they themselves set up. For an openness to diverse documentary strategies shades into the possibility of using the imagery and conventions usually associated with fiction and mass culture generally (as in the work of the Cuban documentary filmmaker Santiago Alvarez).

THE DIALOGIC TEXT

For Solanas and Getino, First Cinema typically constructs self-sufficient 'hermetic structures that are born and die on the screen' (1997:41–2). First Cinema is a 'continuation of nineteenth-century art, of bourgeois art: man is accepted only as a passive and consuming object' (1997:42). Here Solanas and Getino flag one of the recurrent concerns of Third Cinema: to engage and stimulate the spectator in qualitatively different ways to First Cinema. In the latter, spectators are not invited to consider themselves as participants in the making of history. First Cinema draws the spectator into the 'hermetic structures' of the film and severs their social, cultural, political and moral connections with the real world outside the film. In the earlier discussion of *Amistad* (Chapter Three), we found a striking example of this process. The film suggests that the spectator is the passive recipient of historical progress brought about by the struggles of the past. The spectator's relationship to the film and to the making of history would be very different if *Amistad* had suggested the history it represents had not resolved all the problems of humanity and that the seeds of many persistent and contemporaneous problems have been sown in the past, that history is still a site of struggle.

For the makers of *The Hour of the Furnaces*, such a hermetic, self-enclosed structure would be an affront to the audience who were making a political statement by the very act of watching the film within a context of military rule. Solanas and Getino develop the notion of film as a 'detonator' of ideas, as a 'pretext' for gathering together in dangerous conditions. Hence the dividing of the film into discrete chapters could facilitate the film being stopped at any point and the issues raised could be debated. The film *'sought its own liberation in its subordination to and insertion in others, the principal protagonists of life'* (1997:54).

Steve Neale has criticised *The Hour of the Furnaces* and compared it unfavourably to the modernist practices of Godard's cinema. The problem with the film for Neale is that its own position and analysis 'is unchallenged, unquestioned, within the film itself. Debate and discussion can thus *only* be a function of the viewing situation and the nature of the audience itself' (1984:441).

Neale's position represents a dominant one within western cultural theory influenced by the avant-garde of the late 1960s and 1970s. But it is a position that also anticipates the later relativism and textualism of postmodernism. Neale's preference is for cinematic strategies that in effect radically call into question the possibility of articulating truths by argument and evidence, since 'any combination of images and sounds *constructs*, rather than reflects, a meaning and a truth' (1984:440). Only in a theory which has capitulated to relativism could the term 'explain' be used negatively as a description of the film's relationship to the world it represents. While the notion of construction is important to any critical thinking, since it blocks automatic, spontaneous assent, when it becomes (as here and in postmodern theory) inflated to the most important ontological condition of all discourse, then of course the grounds for choosing one *construct* over another (that is, making political choices and decisions) disappears. We need to move beyond simple ontological assertions (the nature of all discourses is that they are constructed) and ask epistemological questions (What does this construct add to our knowledge of the world? What truth value does it have?).

However, the most common negative response from students when confronted with *The Hour of the Furnaces* is governed not by relativism (despite its hegemony within contemporary cultural theory) but the older humanist tradition which relativism seeks to tear down. This tradition is still dominant outside the academy. Neale's theoretical position is that if every position is a construct with no epistemological claims above any other construct, no better relationship to the real world existing independently of the senses, then political commitment must seem arbitrary and suspect. By contrast, for traditional humanism, access to the real world existing independently of the senses (the 'objective' world) is all too easily achieved by experts and professional élites (doctors, journalists, documentary filmmakers) and requires little interrogation of the institutional, cultural and social factors determining their position, methodology and assumptions. Here, knowledge is equated with 'objectivity', that is with rising above partisanship, hovering above social struggles and maintaining a (false) neutrality in relation to them. There is little here of the relativist's scepticism concerning the arbitrary nature of knowledge and truths but here, as with relativism, committed filmmaking must be suspect because it evidently speaks from an acknowledged position.

It is true that *The Hour of the Furnaces* does not draw into its representational field a range of conflicting voices and views, as Third Cinema films often do (*The Battle of Chile*, for example). Nor does it have any self-reflexive ambitions where it draws attention to its own conditions of making meanings within the medium of film. Never-theless, I think Neale is wrong to suggest that debate and discussion are not inscribed into the film but exist only in the viewing situation. This is worth pursuing since what is at stake here is the question of whether films can stake out a position, make a stand, display an evident commitment to causes and ideals and not be considered dogmatic and closed.

The idea of a dialogue between film and audience invokes the work of the Soviet literary theorist Mikhail Bakhtin. He was highly critical of formalistic approaches to language and literature that (like First Cinema) tended to seal the work off from 'the social life of discourse outside the artist's study, discourse in the open spaces of public squares, streets, cities and villages, of social groups, genera-tions and epochs' (1992:259).

In trying to re-ground discourse into everyday life, Bakhtin deployed and developed the idea that language, speech, literature and other forms of communication always exist in an implicit or explicit dialogue with other utterances and languages in circulation. As Bakhtin puts it:

> The living utterance, having taken meaning and shape at a particular historical moment in a socially specific environment, cannot fail to brush up against thousands of living dialogic threads, woven by socio-ideological consciousness around the given object of an utterance; it cannot fail to become an active participant in social dialogue. (Bakhtin, 1992:276)

We cannot then evaluate *The Hour of the Furnaces* by measuring it against a set of avant-garde formal strategies. This is precisely to turn the work into 'a hermetic and self-sufficient whole, one whose elements constitute a closed system presuming nothing beyond themselves' (Bakhtin, 1992:247), an approach which both Bakhtin and Third Cinema reject.

This is not to say that formal questions are unimportant. The chapter structure of the film has already been noted but this is only one aspect of the animating principle that structures the film, which is the modernist practice of montage. The film does not attempt to weave a seamless web of arguments to which the viewer must simply assent. Rather it constructs a patchwork of arguments, some of which are more compelling than others. Nor does it construct a linear chronology, a complete 'history' of Argentina which might very well facilitate a more closed, definitive account.

However, there are other substantive reasons why *The Hour of the Furnaces* may be considered a dialogic text. It is firstly one huge 'rejoinder' (a favourite word of Bakhtin) to Argentine society. It is mercilessly critical of the army, the church, the bourgeoisie, the intelligentsia, the middle class generally, union leaders, politicians, international trade and so on. It is hardly likely that a film that calls into question so many aspects of society is going to encourage a frame of mind in the viewer which will *stop* criticism of the film itself. In response to traditional humanist claims of objectivity, one might ask when was the last time a government report or a news programme encouraged such radical critical thinking about the major institutions of society?

Moreover, this critical stance is not based on displaced anger (the source, for example, of much racism), irrational prejudice or unfounded assumptions but is argued rationally (logically, coherently, contextualised, conceptualised) and backed up with evidence. The film does not specify what the concrete solutions might be to the problems it explores, except in the broadest terms, but it does provide one with enough evidence and arguments to come to some conclusions about what broadly *needs* to be done, even if *how* is a question which the film rightly leaves for the audience to solve in the real world.

Bakhtin argues that the style of a work 'is determined by its inter-relationship with other rejoinders in the same dialogue (in the totality of the conversation)' (1992:274). This asks us to ground the work in its socio-historical context and once we do we can see that the film is a deliberate rejoinder to the traditional humanist pretence of neutrality and objectivity. And this also makes it incompatible with the middle-class luxury which fetishises the deconstruction of language, meaning and (cinematic) communication at a moment of profound social urgency.

ALLEGORY AND SATIRE

But today the social urgency of the times is of an entirely different order. It is the urgency not of social convulsions brought about by large-scale opposition to the rule of capital but rather it is the absence of opposition and the normality with which the current social order has cloaked itself which constitutes the crisis. How does Third Cinema survive when the initial revolutionary context from which it emerged has dissipated? The answer is that it adapts and one strategy which is useful in the long night of the counter-revolution is the deployment of allegory.

Third Cinema's turn to allegory involves two interlinked qualities. An allegorical narrative is one which 'shrinks' a larger social totality, a larger historical narrative, into a smaller story. This is then combined with a second operation, for the larger story is not only compacted, it is also transformed or translated into another story altogether. In order for this transformed story to impart its larger moral and political lessons, the viewer has to decode the story's relationship to the larger issues at hand. Thus an allegorical narrative is suitable for telling a (larger) story in a context in which, for whatever and various reasons, that story might be received with difficulty.

A rare example of such an allegorical film coming out of Hollywood might be the Coen brothers' *The Big Lebowski* (1998). This film may be considered to be an allegory about the 1991 Gulf War. It is set during the War which is played out on the media in the background of the main story. The main story however appears on the surface to be completely unconnected. It involves 'the Dude', an ex-activist turned deeply lethargic dopesmoking relic from the radical 1960s; his unlikely friendship with his bowling partner Walter, a deranged veteran of the Vietnam war, and Mr Lebowski, a millionaire whose wife has apparently been kidnapped. But, like the Gulf War, all is not as it seems. Indeed the film, which is awash with references and allusions to various political ideologies, is partly concerned with the overlaps between apparently antithetical political ideologies and the non-identity between labels and real values. In a glorious fantasy sequence in which a Saddam Hussein lookalike hands the Dude his bowling shoes, we see the Dude performing in a Wagnerian opera (can we relate Wagner to fascism as easily as the west labelled Saddam 'the new Hitler'?), which then blends into a 1930s Busby Berkeley-style choreography of female dancers (Is this a celebration of New Deal collectivity? A 'fascist' aesthetic of mass co-ordination? A patriarchal celebration of the female form whose other side is fear and anxiety? As for the latter issue, the Dude is subsequently pursued by figures wielding huge castrating scissors, an image which then feeds back into the macho posturing involved in war and the symbols of national virility or impotence which seem to be at stake).

Much of the film turns on whether a kidnap has actually taken place and who the perpetrators are and who the victims are – all very urgent questions in relation to the deeply murky politics behind the Gulf War. It transpires that Lebowski, the millionaire who told the Dude that his side lost 'the revolution', is a failed businessman living off his dead wife's fortune and using his new wife's disappearance as an opportunity to embezzle his deceased wife's charitable foundation of one million dollars. The film is an allegorical lesson on how right-wing chauvinism (Walter) is completely unable to comprehend the concealed interests of big business, whether in the case of Mr Lebowski, or the need to control Middle East oil production.

However, the film was neither marketed nor was it received by the professional critics as an allegory about the Gulf War. It was framed instead as a Coen brothers film and another example of their clevei, slightly bizarre reworkings of popular film culture. For allegory to work effectively, the context into which it is received cannot be *so* closed to the larger story it has to tell as to make it unreadable. Within Latin America, where the film industry is relatively less com-modified, where there is a tradition of emblematic, symbolic and non-naturalistic representations (magic realism, for example) and where there is a stronger tradition of organised social unrest, allegory may work more effectively.

Louis R. Vera's film *Miss Amerigua* (1994) shrinks its allegory of Paraguay's transition from military dictatorship to some semblance of democracy down to a small-town setting and transforms its lesson of continuing political corruption into a tale about a beauty contest. As with *Black Flowers*, the question of memory versus repression, of past injustices versus present hopes, looms large. The film begins with Evaristo's happy teenage existence shattered when his father, a peasant and activist, is killed by a local army chief, Augusto Banderas. Evaristo flees the town after wounding Banderas in the face.

After a 20-year ellipsis, the film begins again on the day that the beauty contestants are to be judged. Despite the transition to democracy, Banderas, now a Colonel, effectively runs the town, owning the press and radio station while the local politicians are cowed by him. The beauty contest, which is being visited by digni-taries from the government, is being constructed as a sign of progress, aspiration, democracy and a celebration of the nation. But it is all built on repressing the past while the Colonel seeks to rig the result in favour of Maria, his son's fiancée, in order to give her some status. Evaristo's unexpected re-appearance (he has been fighting on the side of the Sandinistas in Nicaragua) is like the return of the repressed: the wound left on the Colonel's face all those years ago begins to bleed once more. *Miss Amerigua* is an admittedly minor work which does not do justice to the issues it touches on. Evaristo's sister, Rosa, is an interesting figure in this regard. The film touches on the gendered division of political activity which *Black Flowers* explored. The 1970s often saw the men go into underground guerilla fighting, while wives, lovers and mothers were left to grieve, to seek justice for the 'disappeared', to get on with their lives, to feel angry at being left behind, and so on. Some of this resentment as well as amnesia is evident in Rosa, who is sleeping with the Colonel. But how all this complicates Evaristo's relationship with his sister is rapidly sidelined in favour of reuniting him with his teenage love Maria and resolving the problem of the Colonel by having him die in a shoot-out at the beauty contest.

A more substantial allegory can be found in Fernando Solanas's *The Voyage* (1990). As with *Miss Amerigua*, Solanas's film also makes use of satire. The rhetorical strategy of satire is to reveal the absurdity of existing shibboleths and orthodoxies and the pretensions of the powerful. Like allegory, satire is perfectly suited to the current historical conjuncture. For what is more absurd and yet little challenged than the current mania for free market economics?

The Voyage is structured around a series of allegorical and satirical vignettes on the institutional corruption of Latin-American politics and economics, strung together by the journey of 17-year-old Martin, who is searching for his father. The film is very much a pan-American tale, moving from the freezing southern tip of Argentina up to Mexico. This epic structure ('epic' in the Brechtian sense) is interlaced with the comic-strip narratives that Martin's father has drawn and sent to him. The stories are of mythological characters such as the truck driver Americo Incomplete, the boatman Somebody Rows and Tito who bangs an enormous drum which represents the sound of hope in the dark days of dictatorship and, now, neo-liberal economics. Martin will meet many of these characters on his journey, thus heightening the allegorical quality of his particular journey. Just as *The Hour of the Furnaces* uses drawings and portraits to represent the past, so *The Voyage* uses the comic strip to depict aspects of the past, such as examples of early British colonialism.

The film begins on a snowy island off the Argentine mainland where Martin lives with his mother, who is separated from his father, and her new husband with whom Martin continually fights. While the representation of a conflictual family life is naturalistic, the depiction of Martin's school is of a different order. The place appears to be an abandoned facility of some kind (there are no windows, no heating and holes in the roof) where paintings of past military leaders regularly come crashing down off the walls. The education the boys receive is irrelevant to the conditions (both immediate and national) they are living in (a familiar theme from *The Hour of the Furnaces*) and the institution is presided over by the militaristic Garrido who is given to singing, opera-style, as he barks at the students. (This recalls *The Hour of the Furnaces* where opera is played over a scene of a prostitute servicing her shanty-town customers in rural Argentina. The idea of romantic love and powerful feelings conveyed in opera is ironically juxtaposed with the desolate nature of the contract between the prostitute and the men, while also being a critique on the irrelevance of European high culture (so prized by Argentinean élites) to the lives of the poor.)

The allegorical strategy of the film becomes apparent when we see that the island is prone to severe tilting due to 'deregulation'. Here the metaphor of turbulence, of ups and downs associated with market economics, is *literalised* by the tilting island. This strategy is repeated throughout the film. On his travels Martin enters 'New Patagonia', a portion of Argentina that has been sold off to British and American capital for its oil reserves. The metaphor of 'selling the country' is here represented as a literal policy. In Peru, Foreign Debt Collecting trucks roam the countryside and impoverish already impoverished peasants. In Brazil, everyone wears constraining straps and braces which they have to periodically tighten up (a literalisation not only of the saying, 'tightening one's belt' but also a surreal affinity with the Structural Adjustment Programmes run by the International Monetary Fund). In Mexico there is a meeting of the Organisation of Countries on their Knees (a parody of the US-sponsored Organisation of American States) where delegates praise kneeling as the only viable political position in the modern world (and do so of course on their knees). It is worth noting that, unlike *The Big Lebowski*, the marketing of the film on video did make clear that this was a political allegory through an interview with the director on the inside cover.

One of the best set-pieces in the film is presented through Martin's visit to Buenos Aires which strongly recalls the chapter on the port city in *The Hour of the Furnaces*. When Martin arrives looking for his father's parents, he finds the city virtually under water. Navigation is by boat and it is Somebody Rows, who came to Argentina from Chile on 'the tide of '73', who gives Martin a tour. Like the tilting island, the flood waters literalise the dominance of neo-liberalism.

Traditionally, allegory has often used nature for its own signs and meanings, and *The Voyage* is very much in that tradition. In his study of Paris in the nineteenth century, Walter Benjamin was much drawn to the allegorical use of nature in the poetry of Baudelaire. Benjamin's own poetic prose sought to use nature metaphorically to highlight the *historical* dynamics of capital. Here he is commenting on the shopping arcades of the nineteenth century, once at the cutting edge of modernity, but now appearing distinctly quaint in an era of mass culture:

> As rocks of the Miocene or Eocine in places bear the imprint of monstrous creatures from those ages, so today arcades dot the metropolitan landscape like caves containing the fossil remains of a vanished monster: the consumer of the pre-imperial era of capitalism, the last dinosaur of Europe. (Benjamin, 1999b:540)

The notion of the natural fossil is here used to point up the altogether *different* and more rapid historical change promoted by capitalism in contrast to the glacially slow processes of nature. Whereas apologists of capital try to use concepts of a 'natural order' to legitimise the *status quo*, Benjamin, conversely, uses images of nature to point up the gap between capital and nature and to re-sensitise the reader to the peculiarity of this social order and the rapidity of its social transformations. Similarly, *The Voyage* uses nature not to naturalise the social world, but to point to its absurdity and thus to denaturalise it.

This denaturalisation strategy (a classic modernist and Brechtian move) is important because, as the Buenos Aires sequence unfolds, it is clear that despite the bizarre circumstances that people occupy, the 'normal' rules of political and economic life are merely adapted (and therefore continued) rather than repudiated. Now it is plots of water that are being sold instead of land, while others muse on the tourist benefits of selling yourself as the 'Venice of the South'. The media are a prime example of this strategy of adaption and normalisation of the absurd. The tide forecaster on television is a smiling figure telling the audience that in the south the waters will rise only up to the neck, while further south, the waters will exceed nose level (a diagram helpfully illustrates this).

In the heart of Buenos Aires tilted camera shots look up at the gleaming corporate buildings just as they do in *The Hour of the Furnaces*. Martin is overcome with the nausea at the smell of the sewage. As Somebody Rows notes, four million shits a day is a lot of sewage. We see a woman berate the 'Shitman' for not coming the previous day. She is concerned that her boutique is losing business. This recalls the analysis of the *petit bourgeois* in *The Hour of the Furnaces* which notes how this class fraction are always lamenting a world in which change is necessary but impossible.

Passing through the city centre, Martin and Somebody witness the president, Dr Frog, give an impromptu interview with the media. As Dr Frog's name implies, he is the political symbol of adaption (and is dressed in a wet suit and flippers from the waist down). Here we see a satire on the clichés of political discourse and the ineffectual nature of the media. Asked if the waters will subside, Dr Frog replies that they will remain 'just above predicted levels'. He repeats his aspirational campaign slogan ('Argentines, Swim For It!') and asks the media not to 'rock the boat'. He departs to loud applause followed by a retinue of generals, bureaucrats and a bishop.

In *The Hour of the Furnaces* the voice-over which introduces us to Buenos Aires has the upbeat celebratory *tone* of a breathless travelogue. But this tone is counterpointed with the actual *content* of the narrator's speech which is a critical commentary on the class interests that dominate the capital. This is a good example of the dialogic nature of the narrator, using parody to critique the gulf between reality and the discourses that represent the self-perceptions of the élites. It compares interestingly with *The Voyage* which also uses the formulaic recycling of clichés in a new incredibly desperate context to illuminate the irrationality of the context and the inadequacy of the discourses people use.

While acknowledging that the rule of the generals has been replaced by some form of electoral politics, the intertextual references to *The Hour of the Furnaces* suggest fundamental continuities in terms of what is wrong with Latin America. Global capitalism, neo-colonialism and an indigenous bourgeoisie and their political élites set the agenda for life, such as it is. Both films use satire but *The Voyage* also represents a fruitful engagement with popular

culture. However, what is missing from the later film is any substantial sense that things can change. Martin's journey is supposed
to be one of self-discovery, an allegorical comment on Latin America.
At the film's conclusion Martin declares that he has learned he must
help himself. Quite how he has come to this conclusion is a mystery
however since he has been a passive observer of people by and large
passively accepting the absurdity of their situation. The few
moments of resistance we see (an attack on the Foreign Debt
Collecting vans, for example, or a militant priest condemning the
commodification of labour) make no discernible impact on Martin.
To strike a somewhat Lukácsian note, there is little evidence of
Martin interacting in any sustained way with the people he meets,
learning from his experiences and changing as a result. Despite the
surreal quality of the lands he travels through, social relationships
seem as static as in any naturalistic film. In fact, despite the film's
apparently optimistic ending (Martin is reunited with his father),
the film is informed by a profound pessimism. All the personal relationships he and we encounter are transitory, antagonistic or have
already broken up. Third Cinema films should avoid false optimism
and we have already seen in Chapter Three that the historical
tragedy is, by definition, hardly upbeat. But there is little sense in
The Voyage of where change might come from when, even at a
personal level, relationships are shattered and based on betrayal and
selfishness. All this no doubt reflects the very difficult political circumstances of the times, a fact that should be acknowledged while
avoiding the pessimistic conclusion that because the times are
difficult, neither change nor Third Cinema is possible.

GENERIC TRANSFORMATIONS: THE MUSICAL

The first wave of Third Cinema theory and practice in the 1960s may
be characterised as primarily a dialectic between Second Cinema and
Third Cinema, where the latter sought to transform the cultural
expressiveness of art cinema and its partial engagement with
national realities, especially through the documentary genre, into a
cinema of engagement with mass political struggle. However, very
quickly Third Cinema *practice* began to engage with First Cinema
(Humberto Solas's 1969 film *Lucia* was groundbreaking in this
regard) but the *theory* did not develop much beyond its initial
rejection of First Cinema. This bifurcation between theory and

practice has been very costly for a number of reasons. It has meant that Third Cinema films that engage with First Cinema are often not *recognised* as Third Cinema films, which in turn encourages the view that Third Cinema belongs to the past. An engagement with First Cinema is today even more crucial. The cultural and economic hegemony of First Cinema combined with the wider political contraction of revolutionary struggles, demands such an engagement. Such an engagement is not necessarily a compromise for Third Cinema but there are dangers and problems that have to be negotiated. A theoretically informed engagement with First Cinema is more likely to be successful (although of course there are no guarantees and theory is not the same as artistic creativity, although neither is it antithetical to creativity).

A Third Cinema engagement with First Cinema does not involve imposing something external (progressive politics) on to First Cinema. Third Cinema's relationship to popular or mass culture must be a dialectical one which expands and develops its *latent* critical powers and connects its utopianism to forces in actual or potential opposition to capital and class relations. The musical is one such example of mass culture which has a strong utopian sensibility (Dyer, 1981). Another reason why Third Cinema must develop its theoretical appreciation of First Cinema is because, just occasionally, films from within the dominant film industry develop that latent critical potential in a Third Cinema direction and thus demonstrate that an engagement with First Cinema is neither wishful thinking nor necessarily compromising.

A musical like *Evita* reveals some surprising connections with Third Cinema, not least because, with the exception of Oliver Stone, who co-wrote the screenplay, none of the principals involved in the film's production have a track record in making explicitly political, let alone politically radical films.

There are two reasons I think why the film may be considered a flawed example of Third Cinema. First, it was based on the Andrew Lloyd Webber and Tim Rice stage musical, which they began writing in 1974 (although it did not reach the stage until 1978). This historical context is crucial. *Evita* may be set in a socially turbulent Argentina primarily during the late 1930s and 1940s but it can be seen as a coded meditation on Britain in the 1970s. The fierce class conflicts that erupted in the early part of the decade resulted in the working class, and the miners in particular, forcing the then Conservative Prime Minister, Edward Heath, to call an election on the theme of 'Who runs the country?' The answer evidently was not Heath because the Labour Party won the 1974 election on a radical left-wing manifesto. A story about Eva Duarte's struggle to rise from a poor family to become the most powerful woman in Argentina and husband to Colonel Juan Domingo Perón, elected President in 1946 with massive backing from the working class, clearly has some broad resonances with a class-conflicted Britain.

One of the qualities that a Third Cinema text must evince and which Third Cinema theory looks for in all films is this capacity to be *porous* (to use a concept from Benjamin) in relation to the historical context. Porosity is the counterpoint to the hermetic quality of First Cinema which Solanas and Getino complained of. But even First Cinema can be porous. For example, a number of Hollywood westerns in the late 1960s and early 1970s opened their pores to the historical context of Vietnam. *Ulzana's Raid* (Robert Aldrich, 1972) blurs the boundaries between good and bad which had been mapped onto the white man vs. Indian conflict. *The Missouri Breaks* (Arthur Penn, 1976) is more radical, offering a thorough critique (and an extraordinary performance by Marlon Brando) of the violence and sadism lurking behind the mythology of the west.

Surprisingly, the transformation of the stage musical *Evita* into a Hollywood film two decades later not only retains the socially and politically charged qualities of the original but develops them further with the help of the specific qualities of the cinematic medium. The film's crowd scenes bring the masses onto the stage of history in a way that a stage musical will always struggle to do, while the cross-cutting that the film employs brings a ferocity to the social and political conflicts that is, again, specific to the cinematic medium. At the same time, the stage musical also brings something to the film which is unusual within First Cinema. The story has an on-screen narrator in the form of Che and while the musical genre often addresses itself directly and indirectly to the cinema audience (Collins, 1981), the way the narrator is utilised in *Evita* the stage musical, and faithfully reproduced in the film, is unusual and bears some resemblance to Third Cinema modes of address. I will return to this question below.

The second reason why *Evita* may be regarded as a Third Cinema film is generic rather than for reasons of historical context or the interpenetration of two mediums (stage and film). One of the fundamental and persistent problems of First Cinema from a Third

Cinema perspective is that it reduces social and historical problems and issues to individual causes and solutions. This is, for example, a major structural weakness and contradiction of a film like *Panther* (Mario Van Peebles, 1995), which is trying to tell a story of grass roots political struggle within the individualistic framework of the American classical narrative structure. Yet the musical genre generally has a more choral and collective quality. Within First Cinema musicals the community typically pulls together into a harmonious unity in order to put on a show. *Evita* effects a Third Cinema transformation of this choral quality by showing class communities in conflict rather than a single community pulling together. Thus Eva's story is situated within the context of collective forces.

When for example Perón introduces Eva to high society, the song 'Perón's Latest Flame' reveals the resistance which the bourgeoisie and army have to this class interloper And it is clear that it is not just one or two unpleasant individuals who are the problem but the snobbery and prejudice of an *entire class*. The scene begins at a polo game where the Europeanised bourgeoisie have gathered, complete with straw boaters. As they sit around the wine tables, or watch the polo game from the raked seating, they respond *en masse* to Che's questions concerning their attitude towards Eva. Che addresses us the audience and the bourgeoisie address both him and us. When he asks if he can detect a certain 'resistance' to Eva, they turn as one from their conversations and reply to him, 'Precisely. We're glad you noticed.' Then, as the song develops, they collectively address the audience: 'No-one would mind seeing her in Harrods, but behind the jewellery counter, not in front.' Even though Eva and Perón are *in* the scene (and it is to Eva that the film cuts several times as the song unfolds) they do not respond to the collective song and this effectively tells us that these opinions are not actually being openly aired but quietly whispered or tacitly acknowledged. Che's performance here is also interesting. While he adopts the clothes and mannerisms of the upper class for the scene, he is clearly not of them or with them. With that line about the jewellery counter, we cut to a close-up of him looking at the camera, sucking parodically on a cigar and giving us a nod of the head as if to say, 'You can trust them to respond with such a keen sense of their own superiority.'

The scene then shifts to that other crucial social force within Argentinian society: the military. After being introduced by Che, the officer class develop their concerns that she may be getting too powerful and here the lyrics shift away from social snobbery to directly political themes with strong misogynist leanings. The film then uses some shots of rank-and-file army troops on parade as a bridge to a high-class restaurant where the bourgeoisie continue the song as Perón and Eva, in formal dinner attire, make their way to their table. The narrative then develops as we cut to Eva using her platform as a radio star to make a speech attacking successive governments for failing the people of Argentina. The song then continues over the shots of marching troops before cutting to a cabinet meeting where the politicians and the generals pick up the theme that Eva is becoming dangerous. The image track then cuts to shots of Perón and Eva building their power base among the working class (rallies, marches, etc.) and then back again to the worried establishment forces, before concluding with the high-pitched *haute bourgeois* once more: 'Things have reached a pretty pass, when someone pretty lower class, graceless and vulgar, uninspired, can be accepted and admired.'

What is evident here, in the way we move from the polo game to the military, to the cabinet, to Eva and Perón and the unions and back again to the bourgeoisie, is that the musical genre facilitates a certain fluidity of temporal and spatial relations that allows the film to draw these collective forces into a national panorama of conflict. The dynamicism of the sequence lies in the editing. In contrast, the military and bourgeois collectives have rather static arrangements being usually seated within the *mise-en-scène*. But this is suggestive of the rigid class boundaries which they uphold.

It is not just that the film demonstrates an awareness of the class conflicts at play in Argentina which makes it classifiable as a Third Cinema film but the fact that it approaches its heroine with caution and criticism. One reviewer of the film commented that: 'Despite Madonna's impressive performance, we're never remotely tempted to cry for her – and, in the end, that must make the film a failure' (Time Out, 1998:263).

On the contrary, despite using the star system, the film complicates audience identification with the character of Eva so that we do not, in First Cinema fashion, succumb to uncritical sentimentalism. The reviewer's dogmatic attachment to emotional catharsis as the criterion for evaluating the film completely refuses to acknowledge that it is hardly a failure to set out to do something *different*. For clearly the reason that the audience cannot simply identify with the on-screen ego-ideal is because of the role of the narrator, Che. The film opens with Eva's state funeral and huge waves of national mourning and weeping in the streets. This is the mass, public correlate to that private, individual emotional release which the film reviewer clearly yearned for (and which was on such display in Britain after the death of Diana Spencer, so called 'Queen of Hearts'). But within the film, this mourning is called into question by Che who strikes a strongly sceptical note, sitting alone in an empty bar: 'Oh what a circus, what a show. Argentina has gone to town over the death of an actress...we've all gone crazy, mourning all of the day and all of the night.'

Throughout the film Che is a questioning, angry and sarcastic filter through which we assess Eva's rise to power and fame. He questions the extent to which she can be the mother of the nation and the champion of the poor who she has left behind. If the film had been made without Che's narration, then the audience would be offered a much more straightforwardly simple invitation to admire the heroine. Undoubtedly, the film's weakness is that it is not equally critical of Perón and Peronism, a strange mixture of authoritarianism (Perón was an admirer of Mussolini), nationalism (Peronism sought to decrease Argentina's dependence on British and American capital) and socialism (Perón won the working class over with generous social rights and welfare programmes). There is then something of a gender blind-spot to the film in pitching the figure of Che (the authentic revolutionary) against Eva, with her limited social options. Nevertheless, despite this and the fact that some of the details of the historical and political dynamics remain opaque at times, *Evita* is a significant musical and a rare example of Third Cinema coming out of Hollywood.

To contrast Paul Leduc's 1971 film *Reed: Insurgent Mexico*, a drama documentary made in sepia, with his colourful, stylised and lush musical *Dollar Mambo* (1993) is to see very clearly how Third Cinema's dialectic with Second Cinema has shifted over to an engagement with First Cinema and popular culture generally. Despite these formal differences, however, the concerns around cultural expression and military and political domination remain very much in the Third Cinema tradition. The title sequence self-reflexively acknowledges this with a homage to and parody of *The Hour of the Furnaces*. The latter film begins with incendiary slogans and quotes from radicals and revolutionaries around the world, zooming out from the black screen with the bongos as an urgent accompaniment. In *Dollar Mambo*, a similar drum-based soundtrack plays as the credit titles appear, before zooming *backwards* into the black screen. Yet the bright vibrant colours of the titles, and the synthesiser accompanying the drums, suggests rather more conventionally entertaining cultural forms than the stark militancy of *The Hour of the Furnaces*.

This intertextual link with the film that stands as the classic analysis of neo-colonialism is eminently persuasive given the US military invasion of Panama in December 1989. As in the Gulf War, the problem for the US élites was that their sponsored dictator, General Noriega, could no longer be depended on. Noriega appeared to be using inside knowledge of US involvement in drug smuggling to fund counter-revolutionaries in Nicaragua as leverage against US President George Bush (Tisdall, 1991:4). The US intervention involved aerial bombardment, in which several thousand civilians died, although the official US statistics for civilian casualties were less than 300 (Tisdall, 1990:22). The US invasion was only the latest in a long history of influence and control in Panama. US gunboats carved Panama away from Greater Columbia in 1903 and immediately signed a deal with the compliant local élites giving the US exclusive rights to own and control the territory in which the Panama Canal was to be built. With the shadow of its North American neighbour falling so heavily over Panama, and with the interests of Panamanian élites (political, military and commercial) interlocked with US élites, it is unsurprising that the country ranks as being Latin America's most unequal society (Borger, 1999:13).

Dollar Mambo is both a specific response to the 1989 invasion but also, as the film title's juxtaposition of the US currency with the Latin American dance suggests, it is also an allegory of cultural imperialism and cultural domination more generally.

The film is set on the Panama Canal and has two principal locations: a large moored ship that represents the state and the Panama Bar, a cabaret venue. The ship is owned by sleazy-looking gangster types, who are clearly both traders (the ship is stocked with western electronic goods made by Sony, Casio, JVC, AIWA, Pioneer and so on) and involved in 'security' (that is to say they carry guns, there are 'Wanted' posters up on the walls and they have photographs of 'subversives'). While the ship is a place of violence or threatened violence, of drugs, hierarchy and general sleaze, the cabaret bar represents a utopian community. There is no boss or hierarchy of any sort. Whether rehearsing for the show or dancing for the sake of it, the entertainers display a creativity, energy, inclusivity and sensuousness entirely absent from the thuggish characters on the ship.

What makes *Dollar Mambo* peculiar is that there is virtually no dialogue (spoken or sung) in the film. Only at the beginning and end of the film is there a dialogue of sorts between the ventriloquist and his dummy. The dummy wants to talk about 'nothing' but does not equate this with silence, insisting that talking about nothing requires talking about something. Thus we understand that words can be meaningless, insignificant and gloss over the truly important things that need to be communicated. The film itself opts for a different strategy, focusing on movement, gesture, costume and objects as a way of communicating its story.

At the centre of the story is a romance between a black woman who dances at the Panama Bar and a Hispanic man who is a low level dogsbody on the ship. He organises a modest redistribution of wealth by stealing some of the electronic goods stashed in the ship and giving them to the cabaret bar. However, this triggers the disproportionate response of an American invasion. Obviously this is an allegory about how, when western capital is threatened by disruptions in foreign markets, military power can be called upon to restore (their) 'order'. And so the Americans arrive one night to the sound of helicopters and gunfire. The film does not attempt to naturalistically depict the scale of the invasion. Instead we see a dozen or so soldiers descend from ropes, their faces concealed behind gasmasks, and enter the bar where already the women have been transformed into prostitutes serving the invading army. Then we cut to the stage area where the seated soldiers are demanding a show. But the performances are too culturally specific for the soldiers. The Mexican dancers, the fire performers and the tango are all abused and rejected by the Americans, as is the transvestite dancer, complete with a Carmen Miranda-style fruit turban (itself derived from the high priestesses of the *maes de santo*, the dominant black religion of north-eastern Brazil (Hopkins, 1996:13)). This rejection of cultural difference is contrasted with the inter-cultural dynamics between black and Hispanic people within Panama (and Latin America generally) evinced both within the dance troupe and by the romance between the black woman and Hispanic man.

Gradually we see the culture of the invader begin to dominate the *mise-en-scène*. Panning around the bar, we find the bored and homesick soldiers amusing themselves. One looks through photographs of female pin-ups: Rita Hayworth, June Allyson, Madonna;

the American soldier abroad has a long history. Another soldier spins a basketball. A third, dressed in a space suit, floats across the room sprinkling star dust. The stage curtains now have large dollar prints on them. Another soldier plays the national anthem somewhat drunkenly on a trumpet which, together with the cavalry hat, gives an intertextual link to the western genre, frontierism and Manifest Destiny. Grenada 83 is sprayed on an upturned table. Another soldier is doing a line of coke (through the gasmask) before standing up to reveal that he is wearing a tutu. Two other soldiers are fighting, another comes down the stairs on fire and exits immediately while another enters wearing a Darth Vader mask and some silver wings. A toy robot with two faces, one red and monstrous, moves across the floor.

This densely coded *mise-en-scène* where costume and objects are foregrounded as highly significant is reminiscent of Sembene's work. Here a bizarre juxtaposition of signs articulates American popular culture and high culture (ballet) in a context of violence, domination and imperialism. When later the black woman enters the bar, she is confronted by this cocktail of signs and her response – partly amused, partly defiant – reflects the ambivalence of the situation. As the soldiers present her with various cute-looking toys – a battery-operated toy guerrilla with a bell, a balloon with a funny face – she smiles warily, before then becoming aware once more of the underlying threat (they are still wearing their gas masks) in the situation. Then in a brilliant sequence, three soldiers enter, dressed from the waist up, not in army fatigues but the white uniform of the navy. With their athletic synchronised dancing and jazzy musical accompaniment, *Dollar Mambo* is here making an intertextual reference to those 1940s and 1950s musicals (often starring Gene Kelly) based around the army and navy. But unlike *Anchors Aweigh* (George Sidney, 1944), *On the Town* (Stanley Donen, Gene Kelly, 1949) and *South Pacific* (Joshua Logan, 1958), here the music and dance is implicated in relations of unequal power. We watch the sailors/soldiers (a juxtaposition of costume which itself denaturalises both organisations) and like the female protagonist are torn between the innocuous intertextual reference point of the classic musical film and the new context in which it is being *translated*.

At the moment when the Americans make their predatory intentions towards the woman clear, her boyfriend enters. A fight ensues, depicted through dance. Outnumbered, the boyfriend is overpowered and tied up in the dollar curtains, forced to watch as the Americans try and rape the woman. Tricking them into thinking that she will play along with them, she grabs one of their knives and commits suicide. But the way she kills herself is interesting and grotesque. She draws the blade down her chest before ripping open her skin to reveal her innards. The way she makes her body horrific suggests elements of the horror genre with its fascination with the body and its viscera. But here this suicide is clearly a political act. She has made explicit what is implicit in the actions of the Americans, by making herself the horrific other to them because she is already the cultural other who can be treated with contempt.

In the final scene of the film, we return to the cabaret bar. We had earlier seen the American soldiers guarding the boat of the local gangsters which underlines how American imperialism interlocks with the corrupt and exploiting native élites. Now we see the local gangsters at the tables enjoying the cabaret, sniffing cocaine. However, where once the cabaret was an expression of the specificities of local and Latin American culture, now it is dominated by American culture. The stage is dominated by a huge American flag while the costumes have incorporated American iconography (a sailor's uniform, a Stars and Stripes hat replacing the transvestite's former homage to Carmen Miranda). Whatever problems there were in the old cultural imperialism paradigm, to reject it completely is to refuse to see cultural flows and exchanges having *any* relationship with political and economic inequalities and physical coercion. What *Dollar Mambo* reminds us is that if the *context* in which culture is produced and consumed is one of an interlocking national and international domination, then the cultural imperialism model retains much of its legitimacy.

THE VIEWER'S DIALECTIC

One version of Tomás Gutiérrez Alea's work *The Viewer's Dialectic* was published in three parts by *Jump Cut* in the mid-1980s, while a more abridged version was also published in Michael T. Martin's *New Latin American Cinema*. There has however been relatively little *commentary* on Alea's essay (less for example than Espinosa's rather ambiguous notion of 'imperfect cinema') which is a pity since it represents a significant contribution to the theory of Third Cinema. While in parts it is, to its detriment, still influenced by an older and simplistic Marxist paradigm which sees dominant cinema as a realm of 'false illusions' (is there such a thing as a true illusion?) and as a 'substitute for reality' (Alea, 1984:19), the discussion around the concept of spectacle and spectatorship, form and content, emotion and reason, suggests a more complex, indeed dialectical account of cinema.

Alea's essay plays with and interrogates the concept of 'spectacle' and 'spectator'. He understands a spectacle as an interruption in the 'habitual image we have of reality' (1985:48). He is of course primarily concerned with spectacle as the product of artistic work and the act of going to the cinema as a kind of 'interruption' in the flow of life and the film itself as a spectacle. 'The artistic spectacle becomes inserted into the sphere of *everyday* reality (the sphere of what is continuously stable and relatively calm) as an *extraordinary* moment, as a rupture' (1984:21).

But he notes that reality itself can present such 'interruptions' in the form of revolutions, demonstrations or even unusual natural phenomena. In relation to the Cuban revolution, Alea argues that in the initial seizure of power and its immediate aftermath reality itself was a spectacle and it was *almost* sufficient to simply go out and record the deeds and events without having to think very radically about organising the footage since reality itself was visibly and dramatically changing. There is a photograph in Michael Chanan's book *The Cuban Image* which shows people dismantling a Warner Bros sign on top of a cinema (1985:97). Here, reality as spectacle is transforming the site of exhibition for First Cinema spectacles. As spectacle, reality itself is yielding up to the camera the drama of a shift in US–Cuban relations, in the expropriation of private property, in establishing the conditions for the dissemination of new kinds of cinema and so on.

But such punctual moments are by definition short-lived. When the clash of forces subsides and daily routines return (perhaps different routines but routines nonetheless), then the fundamental relations that constitute social reality no longer reside so visibly (if at all) on the surface of life. 'The filmmaker is immersed in a complex milieu,' Alea argues, and so requires 'solid theoretical criteria' in order to understand their world; they cannot simply go out, in the model of the romantic individualist, 'armed with just a camera and their sensibility' (1984:18).

The Marxist distinction between the surface features of social life and its deeper underlying causal and social networks is crucial here. First, as we saw in Chapter Two with Lukács's work, it opens up a critique of naturalistic aesthetics which do not sufficiently penetrate to the fundamental social relations of life (in effect, this was my critique of *Bandit Queen*, for example). Alea's theory of cinematic language is that it is composed of fragments of reality. 'It is not', he suggests, 'just a question of colours, lines, sounds, textures and forms' (1984:21). This is the kind of critical vocabulary of an older art history discourse but such formalism is also the fundamental underpinning of contemporary semiotics, structuralism and post-structuralism, although they use different terms. For Alea, it is a question also 'of objects, persons, situations, gestures, and ways of speaking' (1984:21). These are of course still coded, but they are not just codes, not just images and not just signifiers; they draw their meanings from their embeddedness in actual social practices. A film is composed of multiple fragments of such socially resonant signs which, 'freed from their habitual connotations and daily use...are charged with a new significance within the context of the fiction' (1984:21). Just as Walter Benjamin was interested in the process of quotation as a series of interruptions, as a series of decontextualisations and recontextualisations, so Alea's theory of cinematic signs is also based around the notion of film being a kind of huge quotation assembled out of myriad smaller quotations. The cinematic signs do not start to have a richer, more profound grasp of the real until they are brought into the new relationships with one another.

> Film can relate aspects of reality to other aspects and produce surprises or kinds of associations which in daily reality were dilute and opaque because of their high degree of complexity and because people were saturated with seeing such things in their daily life. (Alea, 1984:21)

And elsewhere:

> ...when we see that reality on the screen, forming part of a spectacle, we see it with new eyes, in another context, and we can't fail to discover new meanings in it. This confrontation and the consequent 'revelation' of new signification are no more than the seed of an attitude of 'strangeness' *vis-à-vis* reality. (Alea, 1985:50)

The question then is not one of any absolute distinctions between kinds of films but of developing the cognitive potential implicit in all filmmaking. Let us just pursue this issue of cognition and knowledge further in relation to the spectator. Alea rejects any simple division between active and passive spectatorship. The act of looking, of observing, 'is a fundamental one' insofar as all knowledge and consciousness has 'as its point of departure the moment of looking (sensory consciousness)' (1985:48). Looking is the means by which the subject appropriates and internalises reality in order to act back upon it. Some spectacles will encourage an internalisation that is critical and questioning, so that the subject acts back upon the world in a way to change it for the better. This of course is the type of spectacle and spectatorship that Third Cinema seeks to foster. So although there is no simple division between active and passive spectatorship, there is a continuum in which some modes of spectatorship are least likely to make connections beyond the hermetic world of the film and others (Third Cinema) where the spectator is more likely to use film 'as a mediation in the process of understanding reality' (Alea, 1985:48).

When people leave the cinema and encounter once again their social and individual lives, what contribution has the film made to encourage the viewer to participate in that social life, to change themselves and their circumstances? In trying to make such a contribution, film cannot simply dress social or political 'content' up in popular forms. This was the strategy of Soviet Socialist Realism and, more recently, of Costa Gavras's political thrillers. This is not to say that popular forms cannot be used – they can, as we have seen – but they cannot simply be added, unreconstructed, to progressive content. They must, to reference Brecht and Benjamin once more, undergo a functional transformation.

The difficulty with simply 'injecting' progressive content into forms whose political implications have not been understood is that it is a strategy which considers form and content to be separate, rather than dialectically related. Formal strategies are crystallisations of *ways* of seeing and so shape the repertoire of meanings around the content. The content, meanwhile, asks questions of the formal strategies deployed: are these formal strategies adequate to the task of representing this complex content?

As Alea argues, separating form and content also sells the audience short and is premised on offering them 'a sort of ideological pap for easy digestion' (1984:20). As we have seen, Third Cinema strives instead for *lucidity*, where complexity and clarity are combined and where the relevance of the spectacle to the audience is felt and understood.

For Alea, a dialectical cinema cannot be one which pronounces truths from on high; it must not hand out 'messages'. For how could the spectator find a space for engagement within such a closed spectacle? Alea calls then for an 'open' spectacle but by 'open' he does not mean 'ambiguity, inconsistency, eclecticism, arbitrariness' (1997:129). This is an important clarification since indeterminacy is the predominant way an 'open' text is understood within a liberal conceptualisation of cultural practices and cultural theory (as we saw with Bhabha and Neale). Such indeterminateness is not compatible with taking a stand, with a partisan cinema. The spectacle must be open in the sense that it encourages the spectator to understand the world as complex and to understand that only through their participation in the world after the cinematic spectacle has finished can the inequalities and injustices of this complex world be addressed. So a dialectical cinema offers a 'path', a 'guide to action', rather than specific or easily achieved solutions. The metaphor of a journey, of travelling, is apt. In First Cinema when the film comes to its conclusion, our journey is felt to be complete. The openness of Third Cinema is primarily an openness towards history as a site of possible action, which means that the film itself is only a staging post on a journey that takes place beyond the cinematic spectacle. It is a spectacle from which the spectator may draw certain conclusions about the nature of the world but not comfort or complacency, either about the world or their own position, ideas or values within it.

This complex, open-ended but committed cinema must address the crucial issue of identification. Within dominant cinema, identification, the involvement of the spectator in the diegetic world of the spectacle, has been strongly based on emotion and used conservatively to shore up established social relations.

I can relate a personal anecdote to illustrate this. I once had a conversation with someone whom I had never met before who was telling me how moved to tears she was by a new prison drama, a Tom Hanks vehicle, *The Green Mile* (2000). I happened to note that despite the film's portrayal of a friendship between a warm-hearted prison guard and a simple black prisoner on death row in the 1930s, America was still executing (mainly black) prisoners today. At which point my interlocutor's head swivelled as she declared that the death sentence was a very good thing and that they should do it 'here' (the UK). So, this spectator had been moved to tears by the film but without any engagement in the issues involved in state killing. Admittedly, *The Green Mile* is a particularly sentimental film but, as we saw in relation to one critic's response to *Evita*, the need to be moved emotionally is the dominant criterion for evaluating films for many people.

Capitalism typically develops our capacities and relationships, *one-sidedly*. A recent report from Worldwatch found that globally nearly 1.2 billion people go hungry every day, while 1.2 billion people suffer from obesity. Thus it is no surprise to find that dominant cinema develops our emotional responses one-sidedly at the expense of our critical faculties. Alea draws on the work of Brecht and Eisenstein to try to formulate a dialectical relation between emotion and reason in cinema. While Brecht favoured reason, it was never at the complete expense of emotional engagement (hence his alienation strategies catapulted the spectator out of the spectacle so that they could reassess the basis of their identifications and pleasures). Eisenstein meanwhile was particularly interested in the pathos involved in the cinematic experience but he also sought to put this emotional stimulation to the service of thinking critically.

Third Cinema cannot reject emotional engagements because without passion, without a sense of anger, there can be no sense of solidarity and no desire to change the world outside the spectacle. Identification with the other on screen is also a process of self-trans-formation 'in which spectators move away from themselves, stop being themselves so as to live within an *other* – in the character. That moment is invested with a special interest insofar as it constitutes the premise of a desirable change' (Alea, 1985:51).

What Alea has spotted here is the *latent* desire for change (and we may add, solidarity) implicit in the process of identification. Because identification is rooted in emotion and feeling it has an immediacy and vividness which makes it so compelling. However, to complete the dialectical circuit, this imaginary transformation of self into the spectacle must then be reconnected with the world outside the spectacle. The film, 'must aid the viewers' return to the other reality – the one which pushed them momentarily to relate themselves to the spectacle to distract themselves, to play' (Alea, 1985:53). It is our rational, reasoning, critical faculties that are best equipped to relativise the spectacle and return it to its proper place as one component of a wider social and historical reality into which it is making a modest intervention.

CUBA AND *THE ELEPHANT AND THE BICYCLE*

Cuba is no island of socialism, no refuge from the contemporary
dominance of capitalism. Prior to the 1959 revolution, Cuba's core
economy was sugar and it was heavily dependent on trade with the
US. A US-led and indeed imposed trade embargo between the west
and Cuba after the revolution effectively forced Cuba into the arms
of the Soviet bloc, with its bureaucracy, inefficiency and lack of
democracy. With the fall of the Berlin Wall in 1989 and the
subsequent implosion of the Soviet Empire, economic aid to this tiny
island ceased altogether. The 1990s have seen Cuban living standards
fall, the expansion of the black market and tourism, with all its
ambiguous effects. These are not the circumstances in which any
revolution can survive. Nor are they the circumstances in which the
official cinema can flourish as Third Cinema. Thus the 'golden age'
of Cuban cinema coincides with the period in which the revolution
made its greatest advances (for example, institutionalising a universal
health care system that puts its vastly richer superpower neighbour,
with its privatised healthcare, to shame). The space for Cuban
cinema to be critical is thus greater when it is dealing with US imperialism, western capitalism or historical representations than it is
when the camera turns its gaze on contemporary Cuban society.
Alea's *Strawberry and Chocolate*, which attempts to deal with
homophobia and machismo in Cuban society, lacks the urgency and
analytical qualities of the films from the late 1960s and 70s.

Juan Carlos Tabio, who co-directed with Alea on *Guantanamera*
(1994) and *Strawberry and Chocolate,* used satire, allegory and farce
to mediate a critical perspective on Cuba in *Plaff* (1988). Tabio's *The
Elephant and the Bicycle* is primarily a historical film, an allegory
about the Cuban revolution, but it also makes some important,
again, allegorised comments on contemporary Cuba. Primarily
though (and this is why it seems an apt film to end with), *The
Elephant and the Bicycle* was Cuba's contribution to the 1995
centenary of cinema. It is an extended, self-reflexive meditation on
cinema and society and has clearly been influenced by Alea's
arguments in 'The Viewer's Dialectic'.

The film is set on the island of La Fe and begins in 1925. In the
schoolhouse, the children are reciting their times tables with the
blind school teacher, Doña Illuminada. When this methodical but
uninspired rote learning comes to an end, Doña Illuminada asks the
children what they want to play. Their attention turns to the cloud

game, where the children imagine what it is that the clouds resemble. A debate and an argument quickly arises as to whether a particular cloud looks like an elephant or a bicycle. This opening scene immediately recalls Alea's argument concerning the importance in film of play, enjoyment and the stimulation of the imagination. The game opens a space for the subjective in a way which the rote learning does not. The film will argue that it is precisely this expansion of imagination, latent in all films, that constitutes cinema's greatest contribution to altering consciousness in a progressive direction.

Just to underline the allegorical importance of this scene, the film's title is inserted just after this opening. With a self-reflexive joke, a narrator introduces himself to us: 'This film starts 15 minutes before I arrive.' The narrator, called the Islander, is returning home, having been imprisoned by the evil Gavilan, the factory owner who runs the island and who lives in a castle from where he observes all its activities. The Islander is returning to marry his girlfriend, Marina, but he also has with him a silent projector and film. Pulled by his horse Robespierre, his wagon and equipment cross the only bridge connecting the island to the mainland. But his arrival has already been noticed by Gavilan (cue 'bad guy' piano motif).

Marina however has had a child out of wedlock and is the subject of much spiteful gossip and resentment from the community. Seeing the Islander return, she goes into hiding, while no-one will tell him what has happened. That evening, the Islander sets up the projector for its first screening. Recalling the previous chapter on the cinematic bandit as a vehicle for social critique and a figure expressing popular resentment against inequality, it is significant that the projected film recycles the Robin Hood legend. The audience within the film watch as the hero joins Robin Hood's men, only to see his love, Cintia, abducted by the evil Sheriff. Cintia is taken to his castle and in response Robin Hood and his men destroy the bridge to stop reinforcements coming to the island.

Already the real audience (as opposed to the reel audience within the film) suspect that the Islander's film is going to comment on life on the island. Not least because the characters in the Robin Hood film are played by the same characters in our film. There is Gavilan, now the evil Sheriff, and Robin Hood is played by Santiago, Marina's brother, who is smuggling guns and explosives onto the island as he prepares for revolution. For the reel audience, who have never seen a film before, the impact of the film is dramatic. The next day in town, a discussion between two women about the film turns on the tension whether film should primarily be concerned with entertainment, pleasure and escapism or reality – the two poles which Alea's essay tries to dialectically re-unite. Then, cued by a drum roll, one of the women, a shopkeeper, in Brechtian fashion steps out of character (puts on some glasses) and delivers an analysis about how film should 'like all artistic manifestations be a reflection of reality. The function of aesthetics is to be an enriching manifestation of the cognitive recognition of man's own reality, giving the keys to its own transformation.'

This Alea-like analysis echoes Birri's own call for a poetics of the transformation of reality. The emphasis on an *enriching manifestation* means that film must not adopt, as naturalist aesthetics does, the position of a passive observation and record of the world. And while the intellectualisation or theory of cinema is essential to understanding it, it is not a substitute for it. Thus the shopkeeper's speech is abruptly and comically halted when a large bunch of bananas is dumped on the counter in front of her.

Meanwhile the Islander has found out that Marina is with a child but when he tries to leave he finds that the bridge, as in the film, has been destroyed. The people persuade him to set up the projector and screen again, even though he has only one film. That night they gather once again to watch the film. Amongst the audience is the island priest who has been warned by the devout Doña Mercedes that the film will bring trouble to the island. But something strange has happened to the film. Now it has sound and the storyline, while broadly the same, has been relocated into a Latin American *mise-en-scène*, with the outlaws now played by native Indians and the authorities transformed into white Spanish colonialists. Here the captain is holding Cintia prisoner and intends to force himself on her. The priest within the reel film in turn comes into conflict with the captain for his brutal treatment of the native Indians.

Thus *The Elephant and the Bicycle* is recognising that within First Cinema there is a tradition of representing popular desires which also recognises inequities perpetrated by brutal authorities. As the real film continues, it becomes clear that the reel film is adapting to and influencing life on the island. The screenings function very much as interruptions into normal life in which real life is transfigured into reel life in such a way as to make the audience reconsider their values. Although they are collectively watching the film mutate and develop, it impacts on them differently according to their situations.

Thus later on when the Spanish captain (now dressed in eighteenth-century clothes) rapes Cintia, the Islander and Santiago realise that Marina's mystery child is the result of her being raped by Gavilan. In town, the women are discussing whether a women should be a social outcast if she has been raped. In a productive ambiguity, it is not clear whether they are discussing Cintia in their film, or Marina in ours. Meanwhile the priest is suffering from a crisis of conscience, his latent concerns about life on the island have been expressed via his identification with the priest (played by the same actor) in the reel film. This illustrates the progressive potential Alea notes in the act of identification which 'constitutes the premise of a desirable change' (1985:51). A later version of the film, now recast in the *mise-en-scène* of the Mexican revolution, provokes Doña Illuminada to recall how her father died in the anti-colonial War of Independence.

As the characters in the real film change, so do they in the reel film, which in turn spurs on change for the spectator. Later, in the reel film, the priest appears wearing bandoliers. He tells his fellow revolutionaries that they must 'change themselves' if they are to change their circumstances, referring specifically to reactionary attitudes to the Cintia/Marina character. As the conflict between the authorities and the people intensifies into revolutionary struggles in reel life, so it does in the real life of the island. But something else is happening. Historical time is being speeded up all around our characters. Coca-cola signs, 1950s cars, modern well-equipped police forces harassing the population: all indicate that we are no longer in 1925. This 'magical realist' chrono-logic is crucial for linking these rather comedic and emblematic characters to the great rhythms of historical change which more naturalistic representations miss.

As we move through historical time in the real film, the reel film also shifts. Now it adopts an appropriately contemporaneous homage to Glauber Rocha's revolutionary films set on the Brazilian *sertão*, with their messianic religious figures (Rocha's 1964 *Black God, White Devil*) and avenging bandits (*Antonio das Mortes* (1969)). Even the language changes to Portuguese as the outlaw leader, once Robin Hood, now dressed like the bandit Corisco from *Antonio das Mortes*, wounds the landowner who comes to disrupt the marriage between Cintia and her lover.

   In real life, Gavilan appears nursing a wounded arm and ordering even fiercer oppression of the islanders as his police force search for Santiago. The revolutionary situation rapidly intensifies. Now reel life and real life are unfolding alongside each other: as the barricades go up, so the Islander hurriedly sets up the projector. There is no time to sit and watch the film because reality itself has become a spectacle and an interruption in the normal routines of life. And, as Alea suggested, in such circumstances the documentary film is uniquely suited to respond to the urgent and immediate dynamics of social life. Thus, *The Elephant and the Bicycle* cuts between the islanders organising their camp, firing at off-screen opponents as explosions erupt all around them, and the reel film which shows documentary archival footage (some of it taken from a film by Alea on the Cuban revolution) of tanks firing their cannons. While all this is going on, Don Prudencio is the one member of the community who thinks that the islanders have gone mad because they keep watching the same film that for him has not changed. This character, who is friends with Gavilan, does not have the imagination to engage dialectically with the film. His name is emblematic of caution, itself linked to a lack of imagination and conservatism.

   The climax to the war comes with an intertextual homage to Eisenstein as Gavilan is cross-cut with the barrel of a huge cannon, just as the machine-gunner is with his weapon in Eisenstein's *October* (1927). The film then turns into an animation of the shell heading towards the islanders. However, the Islander turns his film screen around and we cut back to the shell stopping its tracks and reversing itself back towards Gavilan's castle where it lands explosively.

   In the next scene we see Gavilan leaving in a car, telling Prudencio that 'this won't last', which of course is what the disbelieving bourgeoisie said of the Cuban revolution. The film then shifts into another appropriately contemporaneous and somewhat ironic homage to another cinematic tradition. As we watch dancing agricultural workers and choreographed rows of tractors and engineers singing about the joys of labour ('Work is a treasure') the film both celebrates the energies released by the revolution and references the genre of the Soviet musicals (which were imported after 1959). However, there is a cinematic and social critique going on here as well. The Soviet musicals (unlike the particular example of *Evita*) represent precisely that strategy of filling unreconstructed popular cultural forms with a different content (here Soviet collectivism replaces the American dream) which Alea rejected. And indeed

Cuban cinema generally has rejected this Soviet aesthetic tradition which stretches back to the 1930s. Given that this sequence depicts large-scale mobilisation for social reconstruction, there is perhaps also a critique of the banalities of a political rhetoric of triumphalism, of exhortation and simplistic appeals to unity. For at this very moment the film breaks down and we find ourselves in a modern cinema auditorium with the very characters we had been watching. What we had taken to be the real film has turned out to be just another reel film. In Brechtian fashion this catapults the spectator out into another diegetic layer around which to build its final dialectic for the viewer.

The film projector has broken down but there are no spare parts (a reference to the US trade embargo) and so the disappointed audience leave the cinema. The film cuts to Doña Illuminada (no longer blind, thanks to advances in health care) in the classroom once more. Again she is doing times tables with the children but now, when she asks about the clouds, instead of a game involving the subjective imagination the children stand up and give scientific descriptions of the various types of cloud formations. Once more this is both a cinematic and social comment. It is a cinematic comment on the need for play and entertainment and a social criticism on an overly rationalistic discourse which crushes the very resource which the revolution depended on: the imagination.

When Samuel, the projectionist, solves the problem of the projector by adapting a spare part from the printing machine, he is displaying this vital imaginative resource. The community return to the cinema, anxious to see how the film ends. The lights dim, the projector runs. The camera is positioned in a frontal shot of the audience looking at us, the audience. There is an uncomfortable silence. Then it becomes clear that they (the reel audience) really are looking at us, the real audience. Some of the reel audience stir restlessly and declare that they are bored looking at these people who are looking at them. They start to leave. But Doña Illuminada tells them to wait: she leans forward and declares that she wants to see what they (that is, we) do! This of course is precisely what we, the real audience, demand of the characters: we go to the cinema to see what *they* do. Here, in the film's dialectical conclusion, the classic Third Cinema question is now being posed to the audience, the Cuban audience in the first instance, of *The Elephant and the Bicycle*. And it seems like an apposite question with which to end this book. What will we do?

Bibliography

Alea, T. G. (1984), 'The Viewer's Dialectic, Part One', *Jump Cut*, no.29.
—— (1985), 'The Viewer's Dialectic, Part Two', *Jump Cut*, no.30.
—— T.G. (1986), 'The Viewer's Dialectic, Part Three', *Jump Cut*, no.32.
—— (1997), 'The Viewer's Dialectic', *New Latin American Cinema, Theory, Practices, and Transcontinental Articulations, Volume One* (ed.) Martin, M. T. (Detroit: Wayne State University Press).
Ascherson, N. (1998), 'It's a bad business about the old man', *Observer*, 29 November p. 9.
Anderson, J. L. (1997), *Che Guevara: A Revolutionary Life* (London: Bantam Books).
Baghdadi, R. and Rao, R. (1995), *Talking Films* (New Delhi: Indus/Harper Collins).
Bakhtin M. M. (1992), *The Dialogic Imagination* (ed.) Holquist M. (University of Texas Press: Austin).
Benjamin, W. (1982), 'The Author as Producer', *Thinking Photography* (ed.) Burgin, V. (Basingstoke: Macmillan Press).
—— (1999a), *Illuminations* (London: Pimlico).
—— (1999b), *The Arcades Project* (Massachussetts: Harvard University Press).
Berlin, I. (1963), *Karl Marx* (London: Oxford University Press).
Bhabha, H. K. (1999), 'The Postcolonial and the Postmodern: The Question of Agency', *The Cultural Studies Reader* (ed.) During, S. (London: Routledge).
Birri, F. (1997a), 'Cinema and Underdevelopment', *New Latin American Cinema, Theory, Practices, and Transcontinental Articulations, Volume One.* (ed) Martin, M.T. (Detroit: Wayne State University Press).
—— (1997b) 'For a Nationalist, Realist, Critical and Popular Cinema', *New Latin American Cinema, Theory, Practices, and Transcontinental Articulations, Volume One* (ed.) Martin, M. T. (Detroit: Wayne State University Press).
Boorman, J. (1985), *Money into Light* (London: Faber).
—— (1998), 'The future of film – in black and white', *Guardian 2*, 16 May, p. 4.
Bordwell, D. (1979), 'The Art Cinema as a Mode of Film Practice', *Film Criticism*, vol.4, no.1.
Borger, J. (1999), 'US pulls out of Panama while no one is looking', *Guardian*, 14 December, p. 13.
Brecht, B. (1988), 'Against Georg Lukács', *Aesthetics and Politics* (ed.) Taylor, R. (London: Verso).
Buck-Morss, S. (1989), *The Dialetics of Seeing: Walter Benjamin and the Arcades Project* (MIT Press: Massachusetts).
Burke, J. (1999), 'Guns and saris', *Observer* Magazine, 28 February, pp. 37–43.
Burton, J. (1997), 'Film Artisans and Film Industries in Latin America, 1956–1980: Theoretical and Critical Implications of Variations in Modes of Filmic Production and Consumption', *New Latin American Cinema,*

Theory, Practices, and Transcontinental Articulations, Volume One (ed.)
Martin, M. T. (Detroit: Wayne State University Press).

Chanan, M. (1985), *The Cuban Image* (London: BFI).

Collins, J. (1981), 'Toward Defining a Matrix of the Musical Comedy', *Genre: The Musical* (ed.) Altman, R. (London: Routledge and Kegan Paul).

Cox, A. (2000), 'Lights, camera, election', *Guardian* 2, 26 February, p. 5.

Dagron, A. (1986), 'Argentina: A Huge Case of Censorship', *Argentine Cinema* (ed.) Barnard, T. (Toronto: Nightwood Editions).

Dawson, J. (1971), '*The Battle of Algiers*', *Monthly Film Bulletin*, vol.38, no.447, April, p. 68.

Dorfman, A. (1997), 'On memory and truth', *Amnesty*, July/August, no.84.

Drakakis, J. (1992), *Shakespearean Tragedy* (London: Longman).

Dyer, R. (1981), 'Entertainment and Utopia', *Genre: The Musical* (ed.) Altman, R. (London: Routledge and Kegan Paul).

Eagleton, T. (2000), *The Idea of Culture* (Oxford: Blackwell).

Espinosa, J. G. (1997), 'For an Imperfect Cinema', *New Latin American Cinema, Theory, Practices, and Transcontinental Articulations, Volume One* (ed.) Martin, M. T. (Detroit: Wayne State University Press).

Fanon, F. (1990), *The Wretched of the Earth* (London: Penguin).

French, P. (1995) 'Cinema, nothing to lose but their chains' *Observer*, 19 February, p. 9.

Gabriel, T. H. (1982), *Third Cinema in the Third World* (Ann Arbor MI: UMI Research Press).

—— (1989), 'Third Cinema as Guardian of Popular Memory: Towards a Third Aesthetics', *Questions of Third Cinema* (eds) Pines, J. and Willemen, P. (London: BFI).

Georgakas, D. and Rubenstein, L. (1983), *The Cineaste Interviews: On the Art and Politics of the Cinema* (Chicago: Lake View Press).

Getino, O. (1997), 'Some Notes on the Concept of a "Third Cinema"', *New Latin American Cinema, Theory, Practices, and Transcontinental Articulations, Volume One* (ed.) Martin, M. T. (Detroit: Wayne State University Press).

Gibbons, F. (1999), 'Union leader is traitor in strikers' film', *Guardian*, 2 July, p. 10.

Golding, P. and Harris, P. (eds) (1997), *Beyond Cultural Imperialism* (London: Sage).

Grant, C. (1997), 'Camera Solidaria', *Screen*, vol. 38, no.4, Winter.

Guthmann, E. (1995), 'India's "Bandit Queen" gets even', *San Francisco Chronicle*, 7 July.

Harvey, S. (1980), *May '68 and Film Culture* (London: BFI).

Hess, J.(1993), 'Neo-Realism and New Latin American Cinema: *Bicycle Thieves* and *Blood of the Condor*', *Mediating Two Worlds* (eds) King, J., Lopez, A. M. and Alvarado, M. (London: BFI).

Hill, J. (1997), 'Finding a Form: Politics and Aesthetics in *Fatherland, Hidden Agenda* and *Riff-Raff*', *Agent of Challenge and Defiance: The Films of Ken Loach* (ed.) McKnight, G. (Trowbridge: Flicks Books).

Hobsbawm, E. J. (1969), *Bandits* (London: Weidenfeld and Nicolson).

Hopkins, A. (1996), 'Female Icons and Male Machos: Sense and Sensibility in Latin America', *Latino Nights* (London: Channel Four).

Horwell, V. (1997), 'Mother of all battles', *Guardian* 2, 20 June, p. 9.

Jameson, F. (1992), *Signatures of the Visible* (London: Routledge).

Johnson, R. (1993), 'In the Belly of the Ogre: Cinema and State in Latin America', *Mediating Two Worlds, Cinematic Encounters in the Americas* (eds) King, J., Lopez, A. M. and Alvarado, M. (London: BFI).

Keighron, P. (1998), 'The Politics of Ridicule: Satire and Television', *Dissident Voices, The Politics of Television and Cultural Change* (ed.) Wayne, M. (London: Pluto).

Krespin, A. (1983), '*The Herd* and *Yol*: A Comparative Study', unpublished MA thesis (London: Polytechnic of Central London).

Khanna, R. (1988), '*The Battle of Algiers* and *The Nouba of the Women of Mount Chenoua*: From Third to Fourth Cinema', *Third Text*, Summer, no. 43.

Lenin, V. I. (1978), *Letter to American Workers* (Moscow: Progress Publishers).

Lukács, G. (1978), *Writer and Critic* (London: Merlin Press).

—— (1988), 'Realism in the Balance', *Aesthetics and Politics* (ed.) Taylor, R. (London: Verso).

Lunn, E. (1984), *Marxism and Modernism: An Historical Study of Lukács, Brecht, Benjamin and Adorno* (Berkeley: University of California Press).

Malcolm, D. (1997), 'The wrench revolution', *Guardian 2*, 27 June, p. 9.

Marcus, M. (1986), *Italian Film in the Light of Neorealism* (Princeton: Princeton University Press).

Marx, K. (1967), *Essential Writings of Karl Marx* (ed.) Caute, D. (London: Panther Books).

—— (1983), *Capital, Volume One* (London: Lawrence and Wishart).

—— (1984), *The Eighteenth Brumaire of Louis Bonaparte* (London: Lawrence and Wishart).

Marx, K. and Engels, F. (1989), *The German Ideology* (London: Lawrence and Wishart).

Mèszàros, I. (1995), *Beyond Capital* (London: Merlin Press).

Moore, M. (1999), 'Letter from Mexico', *Washington Post*, 9 December.

Mullin, J. (1998), 'Meet the General', *Guardian 2*, 15 May, p. 6.

Neale, S. (1984), 'Notes and Questions on Political Cinema': *Hour of the Furnaces* and *Ici et ailleurs*', *Show Us Life: Towards a History and Aesthetics of the Committed Documentary* (ed.) Waugh, T. (Metuchen: Scarecrow Press).

Ngangura, M. (1996), 'African Cinema – Militancy or Entertainment?', *African Experiences of Cinema* (ed.) Bakari, I. and Cham, M. (London: BFI).

Peary, D. (1982), *Cult Movies* (London: Vermilion).

Rees, J. (1998), *The Algebra of Revolution, the Dialectic and the Classical Marxist Tradition* (London: Routledge).

Reiss, E. (1997), *Marx, A Clear Guide* (London: Pluto).

Rocha, G. (1997), 'An Esthetic of Hunger', *New Latin American Cinema, Theory, Practices, and Transcontinental Articulations, Volume One* (ed.) Martin, M. T. (Detroit: Wayne State University Press).

Rosenberg, S. (1995), 'Heroine with a vengeance', *San Francisco Examiner*, 7 July.

Sainsbury, P. (1971), 'Editorial', *Afterimage*, Summer, no.3.

Sanjinés, J. (1997), 'Problems of Form and Content in Revolutionary Cinema', *New Latin American Cinema, Theory, Practices, and Transcontinental Articulations, Volume One* (ed.) Martin, M. T. (Detroit: Wayne State University Press).

160   Political Film

Scott, N. (1995), 'Argentina's dark, dirty past refuses to lie down and die', *Guardian*, 23 May, p. 9.

Sen, M. (1994), 'The outlaw', *Guardian* (Features), 8 December, p. 6.

Solanas, F. and Getino, O. (1997), 'Towards a Third Cinema: Notes and Experiences for the Development of a Cinema of Liberation in the Third World', *New Latin American Cinema, Theory, Practices, and Transcontinental Articulations, Volume One* (ed.) Martin, M. T. (Detroit: Wayne State University Press).

Sreberny-Mohammadi, A. (1997), 'The Many Cultural Faces of Imperialism', *Beyond Cultural Imperialism* (eds) Golding, P. and Harris, P. (London: Sage).

Stam, R. and Spence, L. (1985) 'Colonialism, Racism and Representation: An Introduction', *Movies and Methods, Volume 2* (ed.) Nichols, B. (Berkeley: University Of California Press).

Taylor, R. (1984), 'Soviet Socialist Realism and the Cinema Avant-Garde', *Studies in Comparative Communism*, vol.17, nos.3/4.

Time Out (1998), *Time Out Film Guide* (London: Penguin).

Tisdall, S. (1990), 'US accused of hiding deaths', *Guardian*, 8 January, p. 22.

—— (1991), 'The General in his labyrinth', *Guardian* 2, 5 October, p. 4.

Tomlinson, J. (1991), *Cultural Imperialism* (London: Pinter Publishers).

Vertov, D. (1971/2), 'Film Directors, A Revolution', *Screen*, vol.12, no.4.

Willemen, P. (1989), 'The Third Cinema Question: Notes and Reflections', *Questions of Third Cinema* (eds) Pines, J. and Willemen, P. (London: BFI).

Williams, R. (1988), *Keywords: A Vocabulary of Culture and Society* (London: Fontana).

Williams, R. (1998), 'General applause', *Guardian* 2, 29 May, p. 8.

Index

Akomfrah, John, 2
Alea, Tomàs Gutiérrez, 3, 4, 64, 108, 115, 125, 145–52, 153, 154, 155
All The President's Men, 69
allegory, 107, 129–36, 142, 143, 151
Allende, Salvadore, 58, 71–3
Alvarez, Santiago, 125
Amalia, 118
Amber Films, 48–9, 51
Amistad, 3, 60–3, 64, 75, 78, 126
Anchors Aweigh, 144
Antonio das Mortes, 85–6, 154
Ascherson, Neil, 71
Attenborough, Richard, 22
avant-garde, 2, 9–10, 11, 13, 27, 126, 128

Baader-Meinhof, 87
Bakhtin, M.M., 130–1, 133
Bandit Queen, 3, 22, 82, 88, 93–101, 104, 106, 147
Battle of Algiers, 2, 8–23, 34, 35, 37, 43–5, 47, 50, 56–7, 84, 95, 97, 117
Battle of Chile, 3, 72–4, 111, 127
Bazin, André, 55
Benjamin, Walter, 2, 4, 14, 41–7, 53, 109–10, 121–2, 134, 138, 147, 148
Bhabha, Homi K., 114–17, 123, 149
Bhavni Bhavei, 95
Bicycle Thieves, 37–9
Big Lebowski, The, 130–1,133
Bird's Singing, The, 29
Birri, Fernando, 5–6, 7, 16, 29, 58, 78, 125, 153
Black Flowers, 111, 131–2
Black God, White Devil, 154
Black Panthers, 11
Blair, Tony, 30
Blood of the Condor, 78
Boorman, John, 11, 52–6, 101–2

Brando, Marlon, 44, 138,
Brecht, Bertolt, 2, 25, 38, 41–5, 94, 108, 121–2, 134, 148, 150–3, 156
Bresson, Robert, 18
Burn, 44–5, 69, 95
Burton, Julianne, 28–9

Cahiers du Cinéma, 9
Cahill, Martin, 101
Camp de Thiaroye, 3, 15–16, 67–8
Carlyle, Thomas, 31
Chabrol, Claude, 87
Chanan, Michael, 146
Chile: The Obstinate Memory, 111
Coen (brothers), 130–1
Communist Manifesto, 34
Cuba, 151
  revolution, 5, 18, 56, 85, 146, 155

Days of Hope, 51
Devi, Phoolan, 93–4
dialectic, 3, 7, 63–4, 117–18
Dockers, 49–52
Dollar Mambo, 108, 141–5
Dorfman, Ariel, 111–12
Dream On, 49
Duarte, Eva, 138

Eagleton, Terry, 117
Eighteenth Brumaire of Louis Bonaparte, 114
Eisenstein, Sergei, 1, 2, 25, 27, 35–6, 108, 150, 155
Elephant and the Bicycle, The, 4, 29, 108, 151–6
Emerald Forest, The, 11, 52–5, 70, 78, 88, 101, 105
Enemy of the State, 69, 70
Eskiya, 3, 82, 88–93, 101, 102, 105, 106
Evita, 48, 108, 137–41, 150, 155

Excalibur, 53, 101

Face, 85
Fanon, Frantz, 18–21, 39, 83, 87
French, Philip, 101

Gabriel, Teshome, 1, 75–6
Gandhi, 22
Garcia, Manuel, 85
Gavras, Costa, 3, 11, 68–9, 148
General, The, 3, 82, 101–7
German Ideology, The, 7
Getino, Octavio, 4, 6, 56, 79, 108, 118–26, 138
Godard, Jean Luc, 126
Godfather II, 85
Gomez, Sarah, 18
Great Train Robbery, The, 96
Green Mile, The, 149–50
Guantanamera, 151
guerrilla cinema, 3, 56–9, 119
Guevara, Che, 120–1
Güney, Yilmaz, 90, 92
Guzman, Patricio, 3, 111

Hanks, Tom, 149
Hegel, G.W., 63–4
Herd, The, 90, 92
Herod's Law, 80–1, 84
Hill, John, 69
Hobsbawm, Eric, 3, 82–3, 93, 98
Hood, Robin, 86, 152, 154
Horwell, Veronica, 12
Hour of the Furnaces, The, 6, 79, 119, 122, 123, 124, 126, 127–9, 132, 133, 134, 135, 141–2

In Fading Light, 48
Indochine, 3, 75–8
Inside Pinochet's Prisons, 57–9
Irish Republican Army, 87, 104, 106

Jameson, Fredric, 103
Juan Without Clothes, 118

Kelly, Gene, 144
Khanna, Ranjana, 21–2
Klee, Paul, 110
Krespin, A, 92

Kuleshov, Lev, 32, 38

Land and Freedom, 30, 73–4
Last Supper, The, 3, 64–8, 115–16
Leduc, Paul, 141
Lenin, V.I., 25
Loach, Ken, 51
Lucia, 136
Lukács, Georg, 2, 25, 33–9, 41, 44, 46, 49, 67, 136, 146
Lunn, Eugene, 31

Malcolm, Derek, 13
Man Escaped, A, 18
Man With A Movie Camera, 28, 31–2
Mapantsula, 84–5
Marti, José, 85
Marx, Karl, 7, 30, 34, 49, 53, 59, 61, 63–4, 114, 116
Marxism, 27, 28, 30, 34, 117
Marxist, 8, 24, 25, 31, 64, 67, 71, 79, 109, 145, 146
McGovern, Jimmy, 49
Mehta, Ketan, 95
Meyerhold, Vsevolod, 31
Memory, 4, 8, 15, 26, 75–7, 109–12, 131
Mèzàros, I, 59–60
Mirch Masala, 95
Miss Amerigua, 108, 131–2
Missing, 3, 11, 69–70, 78
Missouri Breaks, The, 138
modernism, 27–34, 41–3
Monthly Film Bulletin, 12
Morricone, Ennio, 9
Morris, William, 31

Nada, 87
Nair, Mira, 12
Neale, Steve, 126–8, 149
Noriega, Manuel, 142

O Cangaceiro, 85
October, 35–6, 155
One Way or Another, 18
On The Town, 144

Palestine Liberation Organisation, 87

Panther, 139
Parallax View, The, 69
Pat Garrett and Billy the Kid, 86
Paz, Octavio, 80
Peary, Danny, 44
Peckinpah, Sam, 86
Perón, Isabel, 110
Perón, Juan Domingo, 118, 138
Perónism, 122, 141
Pinochet, Augusto, 30, 57–8, 112
Plaff, 29, 151
Point Blank, 101–3, 105
Pontecorvo, Gillo, 2, 8–12, 17, 19,
    22, 43–5, 69
postcolonial theory, 4, 7, 22–3,
    114–17
postmodernism, 7, 103, 115, 127
Public Enemy, 83

realism, 2, 14, 34–46, 53
    Italian neorealism, 17, 37, 97
    Socialist Realism, 33, 41, 148
Red Brigades, 87
Reed: Insurgent Mexico, 141
Rice, Tim, 137
Rocha, Glauba, 5, 85, 154
Ruskin, John, 31

Said, Edward, 14
Sainsbury, Peter, 9
Salaam Bombay, 12
Salvatore Giuliano, 101
Sandinistas, 132
Sanjinés, Jorge, 29, 55–6, 78–9
Sarajevo, 7
Scarface, 83
Seacoal, 48
Sembene, Ousmane, 3, 15, 37–8, 71,
    141
Sen, Mala, 93, 100
Shahani, Kumar, 94
Solanas, Fernando, 4, 6, 56, 108,
    118–26, 132, 138
Solas, Humberto, 136
Solinas, Franco, 9

South Pacific, 144
Soviet cinema, 5
Soylent Green, 52
Spence, Louise, 9, 17–18, 23
Spencer, Diana, 141
Spielberg, Steven, 3, 60
Spillars, Hortense, 115
Stam, Robert, 9, 17–18, 23
Stone, Oliver, 137
Strawberry and Chocolate, 151
Strike, 1, 68

T. Dan Smith, 49
Tabio, Juan Carlos, 4, 29, 151
Thatcher, Margaret, 54, 112
Thompson, E.P, 4
Three Days of the Condor, 69
Time Out, 12–13, 87
Touki Bouki, 32
tragedy, 67–8
Trotsky, Leon, 10, 30
Turgul, Yavuz, 88

Ulster Volunteer Force, 106
Ulzana's Raid, 138
utopian, 11, 13, 32, 83, 87, 109,
    124, 137, 142

Vera, Louis R., 131
Vertov, Dziga, 2, 25, 28, 29, 31
Villa, Pancho, 85
Voyage, The, 108, 132–6

Weathermen, 87
Weber, Andrew Lloyd, 137
Willemen, Paul, 10, 14, 18, 42, 121
Williams, Raymond, 63

Xala, 37–41, 71
X-Files, The, 69

Yol, 90

Z (Gavras), 69
Zapatistas, 87